Life!
You Wanna Make
Something of It?

D0996202

Life!

You Wanna Make Something of It?

Collected Essays
by
Dr. Tom Costa

Hay House, Inc.
Santa Monica, CA

Hay House, Inc.
501 Santa Monica Boulevard
Santa Monica, CA 90401

A portion of "Autobiography in Five Short Chapters" from "There's a Hole in My Sidewalk" by Portia Nelson. Used by permission of StoneBarn
Publishers, 1360 Ventura Boulevard, #345, Los Angeles, CA 91423, ©1988.

First printing, 1988

ISBN—0-937611-37-9

Library of Congress Catalog Card Number—
88-82324

10 9 8 7 6 5 4 3 2 1

MANUFACTURED IN
THE UNITED STATES OF AMERICA

Contents

v

Life! You Wanna Make Something of It?

Life!
You Wanna Make
Something of It?

Preface

It is generally known that Abraham Lincoln was born in a log cabin. To me, it is more important that he got out of it.

It is known that Eartha Kitt was born in a cotton field. To me, it is more important that she got out of it.

It is known that Sammy Davis, Jr., was born in a ghetto. To me, it is more important that he got out of the ghetto.

For those who do not know, I was born in a small, coal-mining town in southwestern Pennsylvania. To me, it is more important that I got out of it.

How did these people do it? How did I do it? How did WE do it?

By changing one thing—our thinking patterns.

We are not like a tree that is planted in a certain spot in a yard. It cannot move. It cannot say, "I really would like to be somewhere else. I'm tired of this place; it's too hot, too cold. I want to be around more trees."

It cannot move of itself out of its environment where it was placed.

WE CAN!!!

Some birds have to migrate south in the winter. The swallows have to return to San Juan Capistrano each year on March 19, the SAME DATE each year (St. Joseph's Day). If for no other reason than to put on the wonderful show, just after sunrise, they swoop down on the town and all the watching tourists who began their assembly during the night.

WE DON'T!!!

Life! You Wanna Make Something of It?

We are not trees. We are not birds. We are not animals with a lower intelligence quotient.

I have never heard of a dog becoming tired of its home, pulling up stakes and heading west or south.

WE CAN!!!

This is what this book is all about.

Life—He's Made Something of It!

by
Catherine Ponder

In 1973 I felt mystically drawn to Palm Desert, California, to set up my global work. On the surface, Palm Desert seemed a charming village—the kind of place a world-weary writer delights in finding. I expected to live there in quiet retreat, writing my future books and conducting the other phases of my work, while letting the rest of the world go by.

The first local person (and the only metaphysician) to "come calling," to welcome me personally to the desert, was Reverend Tom Costa. I instantly felt as though I had known him all my life.

In that very first conversation he said, "Oh, but you have a Southern accent, and I don't detect a Southern accent in your books."

"There's a reason for that serious oversight," I explained. "I had a Yankee editor, and he just kept cutting it out."

When Tom replied, "Shame on him," I suspected a long-term friendship had just begun.

Little did I realize, as we got acquainted on that sunny afternoon, that Palm Desert (and the surrounding desert communities) would soon explode in growth, and that the area, the Coachella Valley, was destined to become a haven not only for "the rich and famous" but for an ever-growing retired and working population as well.

In the midst of all this activity was Tom and his new congregation, expanding right along with the community's spectacular growth.

Over the years, I have had the pleasure of viewing his progress with pride and prejudice—pride in his success, and feeling somewhat prejudiced in his behalf, because I had known him "when."

I was in the happy throng the night he was ordained. I rejoiced when he received his Doctorate of Religious Science and officially became "Dr. Tom." When his ministry bought its own church building and moved in, that was a "plus" for our entire desert empire. And when I heard he had personally moved into one of the desert's most exclusive country-club conclaves, I thought, "Good for him. He deserves it!" (And I rejoiced once again when he chose to move back into his lovely Palm Desert home a year later.) As my neighbor, he and members of his staff even graciously helped me host parties at the International New Thought Conventions on occasion.

I have continued to marvel as he has found the time and talent to write books, lecture extensively nationwide, and conduct travel tours with his students worldwide. All the while, the success of his local ministry has spread near and far, touching and inspiring countless lives.

So I offer to you this introduction of the author as my "on-the-scene, eyewitness-account" of *his* life, and how he's made something of it.

Not only is this book delightful reading, but Dr.

Tom speaks from experience. As you read his essays (and "listen" to him), you will then be able to take your own life and make something *more* of it, too! I vow to join you in that ever-evolving process.

And so to that former "pourer" who now pours forth the Truth, I say: "Cheers, my friend."

And to you, the reader: "May this book cheer you on—and on—and on."

1

Life!
You Wanna Make
Something of It?

I am confident there is no person who has not used or heard the phrase, "You wanna make something of it?" I remember as a youngster growing up with the town bully growling and yelling this question from the nearest street corner. "Wanna make sumpin' outa it?"

My purpose is to give this question a metaphysical twist: "LIFE! You Wanna Make Something of It?"

I am intrigued by this idea. My mind flashes to the statue of David. I think of Michelangelo (by the way, I'm also Italian!) and the times he chose particular pieces of marble. As an artist and sculptor, he looked at the marble with an eye of a visionary. I am certain that from deep within him some voice said, "Wanna make something out of it?"

Michelangelo envisioned where he would begin chipping away at his marble block. He cut away everything that was not needed in order to reveal his plan, his design of what the young David looked like after he had conquered Goliath.

Michelangelo knew the marble contained a form and a body within it, and he saw the vision. He said that he merely freed the form that was already there.

So, he continued with his chisel in hand, and hacked and chipped away the unnecessary marble, those parts that did not belong to his plan—a form of David. He kept on until all the appropriate chips were down.

(Perhaps it isn't bad when the chips are down!)

It is interesting to note that, of the forty-four carvings that Michelangelo began to sculpt, he fin-

3

ished only fourteen of them.

My own reaction to this news is to wonder why would he stop in the middle of a carving? Why didn't he complete all of them? Could it be that he came to know he could not make something out of the marble after all? Could it be that he lost his vision for that particular design? What detracted him from finishing what he had begun? Was he running out of time or interest in the subject? Was he sidetracked by some other ideas? Was he distracted from his first vision?

Of course, we will never know the answers to these questions. But we can surely apply these questions to our own carving of these intangible things called "life" and "time." We could ask ourselves similar questions as to why we don't finish OUR projects; why we don't complete OUR dreams. Is it time, lack of interest, or being sidetracked; or a combination of all of these?

You may deduce the thought that everything need not be finished. Or that it is okay to change horses in the middle of the proverbial stream. It is all right to change your mind. It is all right to change direction at any time, as long as you do not harm yourself or another person—no harm done that Franz Schubert didn't finish his Eighth Symphony. It stands "complete" as far as I can see.

As I perceive Life, there is this nebulous, intangible thing called Mind, and the things called Time, Tomorrow, the Future, the remainder of this Day— all that are unformed, undesigned, differentiated. They combine together as Life, and there is ever so quietly, sometimes desperately, something calling to us, "Life! Wanna make something out of it?"

We are the designers of our lives; we are the

carvers of our experiences. It is a tremendous step on the pathway to self-discovery when we take full responsibility for everything that we have chosen, formed, carved, or designed out of this thing called our "lives."

Mother Teresa of India made a glorious comment about her life and her work with the poor and the sick. "I am a pencil in the hand of God."

I truly believe this. That is why I always follow her statement with one of my own. "So, we have to be very careful what we write."

Phineas Parkhurst Quimby, a forerunner of new-age thought philosophy, lived in the middle part of the nineteenth century. He said something similar when he said that, at the moment a baby is born, it is a blank slate upon which every person who comes into that baby's life writes something. Personally, I believe that we choose what is to be written on our life blackboard. We draw people to our lives; we choose who writes what, because we have already accepted their ideas. We can choose to erase what is written—the great value of being a pencil in God's hand, rather than a pen—and we can change these things that are on that slate called Mind, Time, and Life.

"When you fail to plan, you plan to fail," Dr. Robert Schuller has said. So, in looking closely at this idea, he is saying that we ARE the masters of our own ships. We can choose to steer our "ship" onto the rocks or out into the open sea. We can choose whichever port we decide to visit. It could be a port of health; it could be a port of lack; it could be a port of pain, of joy, or of healing—it is up to each of us.

With this, there is an idea that the ocean itself

is saying to the one at the helm, "Sail your ship wherever you choose. Wanna make something out of this trip?"

I remember the first time I accompanied my board of trustees into the building in Palm Desert where we were considering to build our new church home. It had been deteriorating for quite some years. The building itself had not been looked after or cared for—the sands of the desert had not been kind to it. But a few dreamers, designers, and I saw through to its core of perfection, through the debris, through all the outer appearances. It took ten huge trash dumpsters to haul away that which did not belong to the design. We knew that something magnificent could and would come from this chaos. Dr. Ernest Holmes, the founder of our philosophy, Science of Mind, wrote, "Out of chaos can come clarity."

One reputable builder told us that we would be better off if we bulldozed the whole structure and started over. But nothing of the existing building would sidetrack me from my vision of what could be. We rebuilt that same structure, and now it is marvelous. We will one day need to build again, but the present space will be of great use. What was once an eyesore grew into being "a sight for sore eyes."

In any event, we rebuilt the edifice to its original perfection—a low desert adobe look with squared pillars along the front. That building said to us, "Here I Am! Wanna make something out of me?" That edifice, which became our church, that dream, that vision, took a great deal of T.L.C.— Time, Love, and Cash!

(The structure was the first church building in the city of Palm Desert, California. It was erected in

1946, when the town was so young that it consisted of very few buildings—just a few houses scattered about the desert floor. This was the church that President Dwight Eisenhower and his wife Mamie frequently attended when they visited their winter home there. Later, the congregation built another magnificent church nearby.)

Is this not reminiscent of the story of the farmer working in the field? One day a man walked by the farmer's field; he stopped and leaned upon the fence. The farmer and the visitor began to chat. Finally, the visitor said to the farmer, "God certainly has blessed you with this land, this beautiful field, and the trees."

"Yes, God has blessed me with this farm," the farmer said, "but you should have seen it when God had it all to Himself."

I love that story because, in essence, it is saying that God works through us. Through the mind of a Beethoven, a Bach, a Brahms, a Mahler, or a Mozart God creates a chorale or composes a symphony. Through the mind of a Van Gogh, a Rembrandt, or a Leonardo, God paints pictures.

To every artist that has ever lived or shall ever live, there is that voice within saying, "Here are the seven colors. Wanna make something out of them?" To the musician or the composer God is saying, "Here are twelve keys. Wanna make something out of them?" To an author, God says, "Here are tens of thousands of words. Wanna make something of them?"

The Great Intelligence that we choose to call "God" needs each of us in human form and mind to use, direct, apply that intelligence, and explore Its creativity. So, God needs to express this intelli-

7

gence just as we need God to express ourselves.

I think of my life when I was holding on to it with a very thin thread. When I was twenty-one years old, in the depths of despair, I felt I had nothing to live for or to look forward to—not even a reason to get up in the morning. There were no dreams within me, no vision of my place in life, nor any future before me. But through all of that inner turmoil, there was a small voice within me, saying, "Tom, here is your life! Wanna make something out of it?"

Ralph Waldo Emerson, who preferred to be called "Waldo Emerson" said a century ago, "Even in the muck and mire of things, something sings." That is a true statement of my life at age twenty-one.

I think often of that time in my life when I thought I had nothing to live for and compare it to my life right now. I am in my middle sixties, and I have EVERYTHING to live for. I have so many plans, dreams, and goals for myself, for my church, for my present and future experience. This book certainly has become something to look forward to and to do. Imagine, "At my age, the sage."

In my ministry, which is now in its fifteenth year, I have found a capability for assisting many people in the act of helping themselves. I have a drawer in my desk filled with written testimonies from many people, including thank-you letters for aiding them—in some cases actually saving them by providing healing ideas. I read these letters at those infrequent times when I think that my ministry is not effective, when I think that I have not done a good job of it or when I believe others may say I am not trying to do my best.

Life! You Wanna Make Something of It?

I read these glorious letters, some of them tear-stained, thanking me for being there to listen, assist, and support them when they had needs. How rewarding it is to me to read these letters over again. How heart-warming it is to remember these people at the time they were passing through those seemingly insurmountable times. Often, my comment to people in the throes of a mental anguish is to say, "Although you may be passing through the valley of the shadow of death, remember, YOU DON'T HAVE TO BUILD A HOUSE THERE!"

I often recall the Jimmy Stewart film, *It's A Wonderful Life*, directed by Frank Capra. It's a story told in flashback. At the beginning we find the lead character, George Bailey, standing on a bridge, preparing to commit suicide. Suddenly, an angel intervenes, coming in the form of an elderly man named "Clarence"—who needs to do some good deed in order to earn his permanent wings. Clarence tells the despondent George how well his life and honesty have influenced many people of his town. But George has forgotten all of these people and moments. So, Clarence asks him to imagine what it might have been like if he, George Bailey, had never been born.

The story flashes back to times when George had been kind and sensitive and to his memories of the good in people—to the times when he had actually saved lives, when he had helped others help themselves. The angel suggests that he ask himself what would have happened to those individuals of his community if he had not been there for each of them at those particular times.

I think often of this story in my ministry, and my coming from age twenty-one—from an insecure, frightened, selfish human being—to becoming a person who has countless testimonies of people who once depended upon me, looked to me, and counted upon me in their low periods of physical and emotional pain. I realize IT IS A WONDERFUL LIFE. I treasure my life now, more than ever before.

In addition, when I think of all that I have experienced in life, even the negative conditions, I know that they have all helped me in my ministry, assisting me to become the wonderful (yes, wonderful!) person that I am this day. My bartending experiences certainly gave me a course in people counseling that was useful later on!

> *(A few years ago, I met a woman at a party with whom I had worked for eight years. She was the cocktail waitress. "Where are you tending bar now?" she asked.*
>
> *"A funny thing happened," I replied. "My life took a turn-around. I studied Science of Mind; I've entered into the ministry of Church of Religious Science. Now I am a minister, and I have my own church in Palm Desert."*
>
> *She did not change her expression one iota when she responded to this news. "You always were, you know.")*

Even in the bar business I was known as a good listener and a giver of sound, practical advice. I was known to take a person's car keys if they were too drunk to drive. I would call someone to come and fetch them and to get them home to bed. I could support people in their seeking for their wishes— never, however, very adept at giving myself such care. Now I look to those times past and at today, and I know it was all part of the preparation for my giving help to people in our church.

Although later I studied psychology and sociology at UCLA, most of what I learned in life or about the pros and cons of Life, came through my bartending experiences.

I recall the first time I tended a bar at Earl Carroll's, in Hollywood. A very famous lady, a movie star, came into the bar one afternoon. She sat down on a stool and ordered a Manhattan. I was so new in the business I did not know how to measure correctly, so I filled her cocktail glass (one of those silly little three-ounce glasses). I saw I had quite a little of the cocktail left over. I was unaware she was watching me as I fumbled around with the extra cocktail. I placed a shot glass beside her drink and poured the remainder of the drink from the mixer into the smaller glass. Then I moved away to the other end of the bar.

"Bartender, what is this?" the lady called to me, pointing to the smaller glass.

"Well, it's the left-over from the mixer," I said, "I didn't know what to do with it. You paid for it, so I poured it out for you."

She cast a very strange look my way—one I had often seen her give to some character in a movie. "How long have you been tending bar, young man?"

"About three weeks," I replied.

"I thought so," she said. "Young man, I have something to say to you. If you keep giving that extra something of yourself—I predict a great future for you."

Then, I had absolutely no idea what she meant. Later on, in retrospect, I realized that in life, you

DO have to give something extra of yourself.

Before I learned that lesson, however, I was afraid to give, perhaps because I was afraid I would lose something. I believed there was not enough of me, or something, to go around. I withheld my love, my joy, my money. We do live in an abundant Universe. Nature is lavish in all that it does. But when we live from an idea of scarcity (or as some minister told me, "Scare City") we cannot grow or expand because we are too afraid that we are going to lose it or run out of it, whatever "it" happens to be. We seem to fear newness. We grow too comfortable in our safety zones.

A designer once told me that every house or apartment is, in a sense, a square box. It is what we place in the box that becomes our "home."

A few years ago, I felt ready for something new in my life experience. I believed myself completely ready for a new adventure in living. Up to that time I had had about fourteen different houses in my life. Every time I moved, I schlepped the same sofa, the same lamps, all the pictures and knick-knacks, the beds, the same tables and chairs. Suddenly, I realized that in dragging the same things along with me to a new house all I was really accomplishing was reassembling the house I had just left. I was recreating the same atmosphere, the only thing being changed was the street address.

In meditation one morning the voice within me said, "Tom, try something new. Buy new things to live with. Leave the old stuff behind!"

I tried to shrug off the idea because I did not dislike all the old stuff. However, the voice returned again each time I became quiet and went within myself to meditate.

Very soon I was driving around my community and somehow I found myself in this very swank new Palm Desert Country Club complex, with a grand beautiful golf course. The next thing I knew I was talking to a salesman and looking at the various condominium models. Suddenly, it seemed to me only minutes, I found myself sitting at a desk signing the purchase and escrow papers for a new condominium.

I had not lived in a condo before. I had not thought I would ever live a lifestyle like that. But I felt right about it at that moment, so I went forward and completed the escrow. When I walked through the model that I had chosen, I kept hearing this voice (that still, small voice within) proclaiming, "Get new things! Build a new experience!"

I heeded that inner voice, that confident knowingness. I bought everything new—and I mean everything—for the condominium. My thinking went along the lines of, "Why should I drag the same things over there?" So, I purchased a new sofa, new beds, new tables, linens and towels that have never been used, dishes that had never been washed. Even new wastebaskets and ashtrays. I progressed from the usual earth tones that I had used before in every home to mauves and whites with accents of black. I even changed my paintings from realism to surrealistic art—a most drastic change for me.

I left everything I owned in the old home and rented it out "as is," including my crystal and antiques, my accumulations of all the various and sundry I had piled up from all the previous homes I had owned. When I moved into the new condo I felt like a visitor for the first few weeks. Despite the views and the peacefulness of the new place, it was strange not to be with my comfortable colors, my old furniture, and my familiar pictures surrounding me.

A year later, however, I wanted to simplify things. So I moved back into the former house, selling the condominium. But it was a glorious feeling of being able to go through that experience of newness. I shall not regret it. I have enjoyed all my homes.

Houses, condos, apartments, are all saying to us, "Here I am, wanna make something out of me?" Whatever, or whoever, is in our home, condo, mobile home, our tent, we have, in truth, selected it all, and accepted it into that "box" called Our Consciousness and into our lives.

Interestingly, when I made my decision to have everything new and to have this new experience, many of my friends and acquaintances couldn't fathom my walking away from all of that Tom Costa memorabilia—my silver, my dishes, my collection of "stuff."

There is that old metaphysical adage, "The best way to get a new wardrobe is to get rid of the old one." How many of us can do that? We tightly hold on to the wide ties when the thin ties are in vogue (the long or short skirts, the wide-bottomed or thinly tapered trousers or slacks). We have held on to the old with the just-in-case-the-style-comes-back type of thinking.

Yet, somewhere deep within our minds we know we must let go of things, those matters that are in the past, those things no longer of value or validity to our present life. "Nature abhors a vacuum," Dr.

Ernest Holmes has said. So, if we want to create something, we have to make room for this new creation.

Too, so many of us do not treat ourselves as well as we do our guests. My large home consists of three bedrooms and three baths. One day I took abrupt notice how everything in the guest bedroom and bath was beautifully coordinated, neat and new. In the bedroom, the furnishings, the colors, the pillows, and the shams looked fresh and new—and matched one another. Then I went into my own bedroom and noted that the linens needed to be replaced. In the bathroom I saw the frazzled towels.

I thought, you are treating your guest better than you are treating yourself! I had two choices. Either move into one of the guest rooms or go out and buy new linens and towels. What I did was a gift to myself. Oh, how good that felt! I was worthy of the good things, too.

Some of us want a new relationship. Yet, it always seems that we have not completed the old one. We are still discussing the previous one, cussing it. We want a new job, but we'll still take our old ideas into the new office. "Well, we always did it that way in the other office."

My personal advice comes from experience and not from theory. Clean out your physical closets (and rooms) and your mental closets (and the rooms of the mind) in order to begin anything anew. I love what Ram Dass meant when he said, "If you think you have arrived spiritually, go visit your parents for a week."

We cannot start our lives anew if we drag the old stuff—old, limiting, negative attitudes and behavior patterns—along with us. Every morning we awaken to Life shouting: "Here I am! A NEW day! Wanna make something of it?"

We have the choice, or not, to make Life a re-run, a re-hash, a re-print of the old belief, attitude, or experience. Listen to your own conversations. Do you like what you hear? Listen to the good voice within you. Try speaking what that voice is telling you to speak.

It is true that I moved back from the condo to the "old" house to live among my varied collections. But because of my experiences at the "Club," I have a different attitude toward them. Now these things do not possess me; I possess them because I KNOW I can leave them behind at any moment. I did it once, and I could do it again.

One idea that has helped me to let go of the past is the concept that no one since their day of birth and alive today, including me, has the same people, same clothes, friends, houses, cars in their lives now.

So we may agree then that people and things move into our life experience only to go out of our life at some point—that clothes, houses, cars, and money come into our lives, to later leave us. The secret, although we all know it, is that you cannot hold onto anything or anyone forever.

Gosh, how we have tried to do that. You can't! Our problems, our misery, our pain begins when we think that we can. Okay, point made!

Now where does this leave us?

Ideally, it leaves us knowing that we take no one and nothing for granted—that always-was, always-is syndrome. If we can know this temporariness of experience, it will remind us to appreciate everything that we do have and can enjoy now. The "smelling the roses as you walk by" idea means to me that you enjoy your friends, and enjoy being a friend. You don't really know how long they will be passing through your life. And the truth is they will pass through sooner or later!

The truth is to enjoy the home that you live in, the clothes that you wear, the job that you have, the money you have—because, remember, this too shall pass through!

In recent years I rediscovered the game of golf. Because the first time I went into the game, I got caught up in the competition, the score, the golf pants, socks and sweaters (in some circles called "golf garb"), and the Country Club, I was not enjoying the game. I had to let go of the other things that stood in the way of the pleasure of the game itself.

Now I am back into golf. I am not in competition, though. Often I do not even bother keeping score. I am not looking for a lower handicap; I am not dreaming of being a Jack Nicklaus; I am now enjoying the game—and it's wonderful! This attitude of mine eliminates potential golf buddies, of course, because many of them are still caught in what I call the "frou-frous" of the sport. Too, there is nothing wrong with that, but I just choose not to do it.

Now, when I have a bad shot, big deal! If I have a good one, it's great! But it matters to me that it really does not matter. Between you and me, and because of my attitude, my golf game has actually improved.

I remember a true story of a man who loved golf. Through an accident he lost an arm. But because of his love of the game, he began to practice playing with one arm. In time, he became quite proficient as a one-arm golfer.

"I just don't understand how you can play with one arm," a fellow player asked him one day.

The man replied with confidence, "I have found that the right attitude and one arm is more effective than playing with the wrong attitude and two!"

That is wisdom.

The motive behind my golf game, and my motive for playing the game of Life, is to enjoy it for all it is worth and for all I am worth.

Dr. Gary Middlecoff, a great golfer, said it all when he said, "If I have a bad hole, really a bad shot, I think to myself, 'well, when I get home, my wife will still love me. She'll have a nice cool drink ready for me, and she'll cook me a fine steak.'"

This is how he handles his blunders. This kind of attitude relieves stress and adds life to your years, as well as years to your life.

To sum it up in one sentence: We can learn to dwell on the wonders of Life instead of the blunders of Life. As with that glorious game of golf, or any other sport for that matter, what is being asked? "Here I am! Wanna make something of it?"

If there is a life activity—a sport, a home, a class, a relationship, a vacation, a job, a bank account, a business, or a philosophy—you can make something of it. You can improve the enjoyment of what you are experiencing and everything that goes with it.

Now when I go out to the first tee, I think of this idea—the great expanse of green fairways, sand traps, and lakes—all of this is saying to me, "Tom, here I am! Wanna make something out of me today?" "Wanna get frustrated?" Be my guest!

"Wanna have fun?" Be my guest!

Whether it is a golf course or a course in college or a course upon which to play the game of Life, a voice without and a voice within is still asking you that same question.

Look at your job. Yes, the one that sometimes drives you up the wall. Remember, in essence, that this job is saying to you, "Wanna make something out of me?" Look at your home—the one with those four walls you are so tired of staring at—paint 'em! Mirror them! Perhaps if you did mirror your walls you could look there to see where lies the real trouble—where the joylessness lies.

Take a look at your body. Go on! Look! There is something within that magnificent Temple of God that says, "Wanna make something out of me?" The mind speaks to the body, and the body listens and responds. Whatever we call our body or feed our body, it will react physically. When something hurts or illness comes to us, the body is speaking out to the mind. What is it saying?

Glance around your world. The entire world is silently screaming to all of its inhabitants, "Wanna make something out of me?" Making something out of *something* is up to you—and me. I like what my friend Dr. Marcus Bach once said, "When God created this Universe, he took some cylindrical objects and threw them into the void and hollered, 'Have a ball!'"

The future of our country and our world is up to us. Each one of us can make a difference. We can have peace marches; we can sing about allowing peace. But it is what we do in our private, personal kitchens—our schools, our offices, our churches and supermarkets—that adds the ingredients to that thing called Peace. It is the way we treat our friends, our neighbors, and ourselves that really counts and creates something wonderful.

Let us, you and I, choose to make a difference. Let us take time to engrave in our time a personal tribute to making our lives the greatest thing that has ever happened to mankind. Let us be kind to ourselves, and to that thing called "man."

That is making something *something!*

2

Many are Called but Few Listen

When I read over again the biblical parable of the laborers in the vineyard, in St. Matthew's gospel (Matthew 20:1-16), I realized the very subtle message within this story and its great importance in calling up from within us our inner wisdom.

The parable is a simple story. A man owns a vineyard, and he hires laborers to work it. Those laborers who were hired early in the morning worked through the day until evening. But in the middle of the morning, the lord master of the fields hired more laborers, all of whom agreed to work for a penny. Then, later in the afternoon, and later on toward evening again, more laborers were hired. A most interesting thing happened, and this is the basis of the story—all of the laborers agreed to work the vineyard for a penny wage, no matter the time of day they were hired.

However, the ones who had worked the whole day began to moan and bewail the injustice of their long hours of work in contrast to those laborers who worked only part of the day or an hour or two late in the day. The part-time workers received equal wage to the full-time workers—one penny (obviously no one had defined "inflation" to the workers).

The lord of the fields came out with the statement: "The first shall be last and the last shall be first, for many are called but few are chosen."

Most of us are acquainted with this statement. But have we looked at the inner, hidden meaning of these words?

What this seems to mean, at least to me, is that each of the laborers, the ones who worked all day and the ones who came later to work at the last hour, all agreed to receive a penny for their tasks.

They agreed to receive equal pay.

In metaphysics, in physical life itself, what you agree with or agree to is what you shall receive. You see, if I agree with the idea that my life is a struggle, then Life will mirror this and indeed manage to be a struggle. What we mentally accept becomes our lives. Is not this a perfect example of cause and effect? That Cause is that thought that you have set into motion as a thought of agreement; and Effect being the result of that Cause, that thought?

People who tell me that they live on a fixed income become furious when I ask them, "Who fixed it?" No matter how we try to change it, a pint will always hold a pint, a quart will always hold a quart. It is the same with the mind. Our thinking determines the quantity and the quality of that which we receive. For that which we receive, or which we experience, is just how much we believe we are entitled to receive *and feel worthy of receiving.*

It seems to boil down to what you are in agreement with.

What are you willing to accept?

Dr. Ernest Holmes in *Science of Mind*, the basic textbook of the Religious Science teaching, writes, "If you took a picture of what you believe and what you have, they will be the same, the identical down to the last farthing." So whatever we design, think about, imagine, or dwell upon in thought and word, the great Law of Life shall create for us. "Life is a mirror to the king or the slave," he said.

Now then, where is the injustice in the parable of the laborers. They all got what they agreed upon: "The last shall be first and the first shall be last."

But the next line, "Many are called but few are chosen." That is the idea that intrigues me the most.

Often I would like to replace the word "chosen" with the word "listen."

Frequently I think of the students of my Science of Mind classes. People sit side by side weekly for the same length of time, many months. They hear the same words from the same teacher; they read the same textbooks and authors; they experience the same lights above, the same floor under them, the ceiling over them, etc. But at the end of the semester, one of these persons will have changed his or her life, but the other person still sits in their same environment, their same problem, and their same condition of thought.

I have questioned this variable often. I have wondered if there was something wrong with me, the teacher? Or, was there something wrong with the textbook or the philosophy, possibly even the room in which we sat? Or is it that many are called to the classroom in order to try the methods of the philosophy for awhile but not all are truly listening. Can it be that they hear with the instrument of their bodies, the ears, but don't choose to listen with their minds and hearts?

I have seen young people come into Science of Mind and latch on to the program right away. Their lives are transformed. I have observed others, whom I equate with the laborers in the vineyard, who have worked all the day long; they receive very little out of the teaching, although they may perhaps have labored through all the metaphysical books and classes.

Are they listening? Or are these people closing out the ideas that can change their lives? Do they think that it works for someone else, but it is not for them?

One young man wrote me a testimonial letter saying how this teaching changed his life, but only after he realized that I, as teacher, gave him the tools necessary. However, he found he had to do the digging—the learning on his own.

There is always that Law of Agreement in action, "Whatever you are in agreement with, be it pain, be it misery, be it joy, or love, it shall be provided." Whatever you think (or believe) you are entitled to receive—you shall receive. This is an echo of what the great teacher, Jesus, said, "We have eyes that do not see and ears that do not hear." To a minister, and to a teacher, that can mean that just because people are sitting before you hearing with their ears does not mean they are listening to or picking up the message you are giving.

Many people read the myriad of "how-to" books and become associated with motivational speakers and churches. Too often, however, they believe that the other person or thing has to change. They want their spouse to change—their children to change or their work to change—all the while they want to remain exactly the same. It doesn't work that way!

There is that old example of complaining to the psychiatrist that the spouse or someone else in their life is totally responsible for their unhappiness. "Well, then, why don't you send THEM in and we will fix them up," the psychiatrist says. "Then *you'll* be all right."

"Everyone wants the world to change but no one wants to change," Leo Tolstoy has said. That was the theme of my own life experience for many years. I believed that the only way my life would change is if other people would change their attitudes and habits. I strongly believed—and urged upon others—that they needed to change their prejudices, their likes and their dislikes. Again, I know from experience that it just does not work that way.

I realized that, as I changed my thinking, MY world would change because what I thought of the world became my world. It was, indeed, a great step for mankind in the form of Tom Costa. If I had learned this earlier in my life, it would have saved me so much grief; it would have saved the world a great deal of grief. I find it more rewarding to give the world joy and happiness than provide it with more grief—it has enough of that!

It was an enormous step in my growth when I realized I no longer had to sit at the "kiddies' table" in life; that I was a reasonably mature adult, needing NO adult supervision other than the protection of my own thoughts. WHEW!

It was then I learned to keep the "blame" finger down. I rarely use it, if ever. And even at those times when I choose to point blame I feel silly—I know better!

When counseling a drug addict some years ago, he summed up not only his life but my life when he said, "Up until the time I came in here for treatment, I did not know I had choices, I didn't know there was another way to go." He indicated he would do all that he could to maintain kind thoughts toward himself. "I need to listen to the YES voice inside me—that voice now talks louder than the NO voice." So far, so good.

When I found there was another way to think, other ways to choose how to act and react and ways to love, doors opened for me both ways—good poured in, and good poured out. I know that I shall always have the power of choice to move on to the pathway to self-discovery, self-acceptance, self-love, self-dignity. Or I can choose to return to my self-inflicted prison, my self-maintained pain, my self-sustained unhappiness.

I can think back to the day when a young lady came into my life for exactly three weeks. She took me to Grauman's Chinese Theater on Hollywood Boulevard to hear a grand speaker, Dr. Harry Douglas Smith.

Dr. Smith spoke in a simple, inspiring way, saying very lovingly, and yet firmly, "Change your thinking, and you change your life. You have nothing else to change."

There were two thousand people the day I first attended Dr. Smith's lecture. I wonder now how many people were "called" to hear that service and how many people have "listened" since. How many people, with me, went on to study the Mind and the Self, to attend Science of Mind classes and new-thought seminars, to listen to spiritual development tapes, and finally to have an opportunity to build a church.

Someone reading these words right now could be (I repeat, COULD be) one of the greatest metaphysical teachers who ever lived. Let us remember, it is written that Jesus said, "You, too, can do greater works, if you but believe." He said that he did not have a monopoly on performing miracles. All miracles are up to the believer in the Self, the Source of all Good, the Universal Power. How many people listen?

How many people hear that still, small voice inside and move on in their lives to great studies to become a renowned teacher, a minister, a rabbi, and to have a great impact on the world?

Years ago, I came into the realization that when I attend a class or a seminar or read a book or listen to a spiritual recording, three words sum up my reaction to these studies of the Self and of the Mind, and these are: THIS MEANS ME!

I do not read, study, or listen for anyone else; I listen for me and for my growth, my expansion, my edification. But it takes dedication, discipline, and diligence.

Diligence. I had never used the word very much in my daily vocabulary. Then a few years ago, I was invited to Kingston, Jamaica, to speak for my colleague, Reverend Elma Lumsden, who has performed fine work in Religious Science there. When I was ushered into her church we walked to the podium. On her pulpit there was inscribed the word, DILIGENCE.

I thought that was a strange word to be visible to a listening audience, because it was something that everyone could see from every seat in the auditorium. Then I recognized the wisdom of this grand lady placing that word where everyone could be reminded that diligence IS the key to worship, to prayer, to study, to growth, to self-awareness.

Transforming these lectures from the spoken word to the form of the essay has required my diligence. To expand on the ideas I have talked about so that they have greater meaning for readers, I have called upon the larger vocabulary that is within, that part of me that I do not use as often as I could. I have had to listen to the voice within me so that I could better state in writing that which I have spoken. Diligence. To grow strong in our spiritual faith and activity, we have to hear with a dedicated ear and listen. This is diligence.

Diligence means persevering application; it means persistent effort. What better reminder than the word diligence for people listening to the Word, the Message, the Truth; to discipline themselves to apply principles being taught diligently, with persistent effort, with perseverance.

"Many are called but few listen," this echoes one of Tom Costa's Universal Laws to Understanding: Nobody hears anything worthy who does not listen diligently.

3

Perfectly Imperfect

Is anyone perfect?

I recently visited with a lady known for her perfect housekeeping habits. She was a real "Craig's Wife," all right.

(Craig's Wife, a play by George Kelly nearly fifty years ago, portrayed a marriage going on the rocks because the wife kept such a pristine house; the husband decided not to live in it—it would never be a "home.")

In any case, returning to my visit with the lady, in the twenty minutes I was in her living room, she emptied the ash tray three times—and I don't smoke! Her action would seem to be the epitome of perfectionism.

Many people live their lives looking for the gold medals, the kudos, the accolades, constantly seeking the approval of others. The perfectionist lives by the axiom: "I must perform perfectly or I shall perish."

That may be true if you are a parachute jumper, but it certainly is not true of the average person, or the above or below average person (whatever that is!). There is no way to please a perfectionist. Such a person carries a most heavy burden having to live in a world which, by all appearances, has few things running smoothly or going right. I've never tried to please a perfectionist.

No one is perfect in this physical world. No one ever was or ever shall be. I cite the story of the anger that Jesus, the great master, expressed when he saw the temple being used for the wrong reason. Even he had "imperfect" moments.

Doctors have told me that migraine headaches, in their opinion, are the result of an attempt to be perfect. In the sufferer's mental drive, which is an attempt to be perfect in all things, tension and pressure build up and a severe headache follows. It may last for hours, days, or even weeks.

I find there just are not that many gold, silver, or bronze medals being passed out in this world for Olympian perfectionism. In fact, I would not mind passing out medals to many people for the challenge and accomplishment when taking up opportunity with their imperfectionism. Many persons, I find, do extremely well in their position at home, at work, or in relationships; these imperfect people are very successful being themselves, caring and humane.

I wish to help you, and also myself, to realize that we are not perfect; and that is (perfectly) all right. When we seek to be perfect, to act, react, speak, or remain silent in a perfected manner, we run into mental, spiritual, and emotional trouble. Many times, metaphysicians use affirmations based on the idea of being perfect: "Be ye perfect as your Father in Heaven is perfect." So essentially they affirm, "I am perfect. I am perfect." Meanwhile, there is something within them that is saying, "Who are you kidding? Look at your life, look at your bank book, look at your X-rays."

A metaphysician or a mind practitioner may tell us, "All is perfect, whole, and complete," but appearances show us otherwise. However, the meaning of this is that chaos, the imperfect state we may be having in our experience, is in reality operating perfectly, according to a Divine Law, a Universal Law of Thought.

Now, even though these statements are about us as human beings making progress in life and chang-

34

ing our lives, it is not incongruous to admit our imperfections. In fact, it is spiritually and emotionally healthy to do so because, upon the admission of imperfection, we are at a place where we can begin to improve and change our lives.

The Apostle Paul said something to the effect that we are striving toward perfection, but we never quite reach it. I heaved a great sigh of relief when I read that, and a greater sigh when I understood the concept. It amazes me still how many people reacted when I first used the idea as an affirmation, "I am perfectly imperfect." I saw people, in their body language, cringe, even jolt—there was a vibration of "whaaaaaaat?" But as soon as it was openly discussed there was a feeling of relaxation, more self-acceptance and many "I sees!" When I discussed these ideas on national television I received many letters from fellow metaphysicians, most of whom said the same thing. "It is nice to know that we can be imperfect. Whew!"

Who would want a perfect mate? Do you really want your children to be absolutely perfect? I love my dogs; they are "perfectly wonderful" and important in a part of my life. But once in a while, they slip—and I clean it up. AND I still love them.

Anyone who is looking for a perfect friend is at the same time looking for loneliness because there isn't that rare breed of perfect friend running loose on this planet. Annually we observe the Nobel Committee attempt to richly praise several "perfect persons" in many categories of arts and sciences. Are these noble Nobel winners perfect friends to someone? Are they perfect at all?

Sometimes, we find what we consider to be the perfect car, but somewhere down the road, it will need maintenance and repair. We find the "perfect" house, but it is not too long before the roof needs repair, or the bathroom needs new tiles, or the disposal needs fixing. Nothing IS perfect, and if something appears perfect it will not remain so— and that is (perfectly) all right. At this moment I am reminded of the sweet little old New England lady who could not easily accept praise for her magnificent cooking. She prepared wonderful meals, and every time a comment was made by family or friend, such as, "Etta, this chicken casserole of yours is positively perfection," she would demur the compliment with, "I think it wants salt!"

What we have here is that when something of ours, or about us, is perfect, we cannot accept the statement. Now, that is strange.

Let us imagine having the perfect secretary, someone who doesn't need an eraser at the end of the pencil. Let us imagine a clerical assistant who doesn't need a backspace key on the typewriter. Think of the perfect situation of having someone in your office who knows where everything is and can retrieve it at a moment's notice.

However, looking at this conversely, we certainly do not want a secretary who never gets anything right, a clerical assistant who constantly makes mistakes, or a file clerk who cannot find a file. In reality it is the "happy medium" of a person for which we look. One with whom we can work and be with pleasantly for most hours.

Golf, as you know, is one of my favorite forms of recreation, and I enjoy it so much more now that I realize and acknowledge that my game is not perfect and will never be. It is perfectly imperfect. However, I notice some of my golf buddies, when making a truly great, out of the ordinary shot—for them a "perfect" drive or pitch—find it very difficult (like the sweet New England cook) to accept their good fortune. "I can't believe it," they shout, rather than say, "Thank you." They hedge their sudden moment of glory and apologize: "Well, if I had just taken the 7-iron instead of the 8-iron; if I had used my driver, it would have gone much farther."

Now I enjoy my golf game all the more, despite the score. With my schedule, I just don't have time to spend on a driving range to practice. So now, when people ask me about my game, I say, "I had some great shots, and I also had some not-so-great shots."

Is this not also true of our lives? We have done some glorious things, and we, all of us, have created a good many not-so-glorious things. Let us not browbeat ourselves because we are not number ONE!

(In truth, we are all number ONE, because we are ONE with all things.)

It is interesting to watch Saturday afternoon football games on television. Many of the players put up a "We're-number-one!" sign because they scored a touchdown or have upset a highly favored team. They are calling attention to their perfectly imperfect game—if it had been perfect they would not have needed the umpires with their whistles.

I have said many times that I do not want to be the best minister, teacher, or writer in the world. But I do wish to be the very best that I *can be* at any of these things. How about you?

Now all this is not to accuse you of not trying your very best. But it doesn't mean you cannot improve yourself. It doesn't mean that you just resign yourself to your lot in life. What this does mean is that you *can* start to build something on your lot! It means that just as a rosebud is perfect at a particular stage of growth, wherever you are now is perfect and right for you on your path to wherever or whatever you are directing your mind and your life.

Emmett Fox has an interesting viewpoint of the right and true place: "Many people pray for their right place but in essence, the right place is right where you are right now and the true place is where you are moving towards."

In other words, the problem you are experiencing right now is your right place—that valley of Life is your right place, but it is not your true place. Moving through and out of the valley's problems is your true place.

How many marriages, relationships, or friendships would be improved if we began to accept the partner as being perfectly imperfect? I wonder if the divorce rate would be lower if the imperfections were not dwelt upon, but accepted as all right, A-Okay, just for now.

I recall a lady in a consultation whose main complaint about her life was that her husband splashed water on the vanity mirror in the bathroom when he washed his face or shaved. Everything else, such as being a good provider or not cheating on her, his not being a gambler, or a drinker, or a smoker, was forgotten. This one irritating habit was her nemesis, and it affected her marriage considerably. In our discussion I reminded her that, if there were divorce or a transition—his death—she would be quite free of the task of having to clean the water marks on the vanity mirror. I asked her if this was what she really wanted.

She came to realize that she was very fortunate in her choice of mate. She acknowledged that her criticism of him was certainly an imperfection of hers not his. This one idea assisted the marriage to a smooth course and enhanced the relationship of both persons. The love that was always there resurfaced. She later shared with me that now, when she daily wipes away her husband's water marks from the mirror, she actually gives thanks for them! I know couples whose rocky marriages rest on the fact that neither spouse is inclined to take out the garbage to the dumpster. Each waits until they hear the roar of the garbage truck in the alley. Then there is shouting and screaming while each grabs the garbage bags and waste baskets to get to the dumpster in time. This reminds me of the quote, "None is so blind as he who cannot see." Something like this brings tears to my eyes.

Often people say to me, "Dr. Tom, I just didn't expect that of you. You're a minister!" I then remind them that I am human also; I am NOT infallible, and I certainly expect flexibility in attitudes in what people think of me. I have been criticized occasionally for becoming emotional on the pulpit, especially when a little (or large) tear might fall down my cheeks. "You, a 'man of the cloth,' crying on the pulpit—a grown man!"

"Yes," I answer. "Those are God-made tears, and I, as a grown man of the cloth, sometimes have to use my cloth to wipe my tears. So, sue me!"

There are women in consultations who break down because they are so weary of being brave—so tired of being in charge of everything. They are so exhausted from the strain of being strong at all

times. Because they are expected to be perfect in the
eyes of their spouse, their children, their relatives
and friends, they are never allowed to "weaken."
Many have sobbed that they would love to scream,
"I am not strong. I'm really weak!"

These women with perfect hair-dos and perfectly coordinated wardrobes have, in that unseen
part of themselves, what seems to be the "iceberg,"
that perfect-in-control human under all conditions,
but are anything but stoic. That perfection is per-
ceived only in the eyes of the beholder. Many
women, and quite a few men, have lived their entire lives behind a facade.

One of the first steps to happiness is to be honest
with yourself. Just as William Shakespeare wrote,
"This above all, to thine own self be true." Anne
Morrow Lindbergh said something that has helped
me to attempt to be as sincere as I could possibly
be: "The most exhausting thing in life is to be insin-
cere." But still, there are some situations in life
when we may need to simply exhaust ourselves temporarily. Just don't make it a practice.

I am certain that all of us can relate to that
idea. One of the "secrets of my success" as a minister is that I speak and write of things not from theory, but from my own experience. At ministerial
conferences, we are told that this is unwise. But for
me, however, it works. People know a phony. Even
your dogs know when you are being phony. ("I'll
take you out for a walk right after I go to this appointment." They know the truth!)

Years ago when I first went to Hollywood,
California, I wanted so much, even desperately, to
be a part of the "Hollywood scene." The group I
traveled around with were what I now call

"pseudo-intellectuals." We talked about theater, about books, about "great films"—we never talked about plain old movies—and about exotic, faraway places with strange sounding names most of us had yet to see. We drank martinis before dinner, the correct wine with dinner, the very best cognac after dinner. Before too long I was slowly turning into an intellectual drunk.

Fortunately, I retrieved myself, my life—my very soul—from the attempt to keep up with the "Joneses."

We have to set our own standards, our own code of ethics to abide by, our own morals. We cannot live well going with, and living by, standards established by someone else when we know deep within that those standards and codes of others do not fit us. If we do, we become a squared peg in a round hole.

When I saw the light, I ceased living up to other people's standards and the expectations of others. I took charge of my life experience. There was confusion of the most perfect kind during this time of re-creating the belief system that was to become the true me. Wayne Dyer says, "One of the first steps to happiness is to lower your expectations of other people." But that doesn't mean you then lower your expectations for yourself.

It was with a sudden jolt of recognition that I no longer felt I needed to sit at the kiddies' table any longer—that I had matured enough to realize that I did have something to say, something to give, something to contribute, not only to my life but from my life to the lives of others and to the world.

Recently, I read something I aligned with so very much. I read that "Great men do not do great things; they do simple things because they are impelled to do them. And what they do makes them great." Thomas Edison's life is a good example of this. He didn't create the light bulb in order to become great. He did what he was impelled to do, and what he did made him great. Composers, artists and craftsmen do not do their creative work in order to be remembered for their greatness. They allow this creativity to come forth. The result of their work makes them great, and they are remembered for their artistry, for applying their talent to their vision.

My particular life philosophy is called Religious Science, and its teaching is Science of Mind. This philosophy and teaching changed my life, and because it did that, I have been propelled, compelled, and impelled to teach it to others. If that impulsion causes me to be great, the greatness is the result but it's not the purpose.

Our purpose here is not to set the world on fire with our goals and our dreams. We are here to set on fire that spark of life that is God within us. And if the world sees our spark and our light, that is great! If they don't, that is perfectly all right. Paraphrasing the teacher Jesus, we can say, "Let your own light shine, and set that light on top of the mountain so that it may be seen and people will emulate that light."

However, there are people who are blinded by the light. Or they will try to douse it. My spiritual light has a rheostat on it that responds to my thinking, to my self-esteem, to my level of self-dignity and self-love. I know when my light is set on high, absolutely no one can touch it or change it but me. This is also true when my light is on the opposite setting, the minus setting. I am the only one to turn my light up or down. I say to people lovingly, but very firmly with sincerity, "Keep your hands off my spiritual rheostat."

All of this can take place and all of this can happen when you realize that you are perfectly imperfect on this journey, this road to wherever you choose to go. Accept imperfections, just don't resign yourself to them. Accept yourself exactly as you are now, then proceed forward from there, making those changes that suit you and your world. We need to acknowledge the great differences between acceptance and resignation.

Acceptance is that moment you admit the truth of where you are, and then you begin your path from there. On the other hand, resignation is that moment you accept the truth of just where you are and make the decision to stay just where you are. Both are, in essence, Life affirmations, although one may lead to negative conditions and experience. I believe in affirmations. Here, I give you a list of affirmations for you to repeat daily, if you choose to accept your perfect imperfections:

I affirm I am perfectly imperfect.

I accept my imperfections.

I am not perfect, but I am on a pathway toward it.

I realize no one else is perfect.

I accept the imperfections of others.

I do not expect perfection in my spouse, my relatives, my children, my in-laws, my neighbors, my minister, my friends, my fellow workers, and even my pets.

I accept all people, places, and things just as they are!

I accept people, places, and things exactly as they choose to be.

I am perfectly imperfect! And I accept that right now, at this perfect time.

I accept this perfect place now, and I accept myself in it.

And so it is.

4

The Blessing
of Delay

When first I came upon the idea, "the blessing of delay," and then used it as a theme for a lecture, there was quite an array of reactions and questions. I admit to feeling some disquietude about it.

I believe this was due mainly to all of these motivational books we read—all those "how-to-be-successful-now" articles and essays that adorn the popular magazines, and certainly the talks we hear weekly in our churches and lecture halls. And perhaps, too, all of the "you-can-have-it-all-immediately" seminars. Still, despite these many motivational movements, organizations, and churches—all seeming to say exactly what the teacher Jesus said: "The Kingdom of Heaven is at hand." There is that little voice within speaking out at the same moment saying, "Okay, but it certainly isn't here yet." "It's got to be in someone else's kingdom," or "I know that the fields are white with harvest, but why can't I have my share now?"

I once heard the great teacher and author, Dr. Catherine Ponder, explain this idea: "In every delay there's a blessing on its way." My insides flipped when I heard that statement. It was said to me at a time in my life when I wanted a specific something, and I wanted it NOW! However, after the initial shock of taking in that unusual idea, I began to analyze and watch the blessings of many delays that happened later in my life. Actually, there were things that I wanted but for which I now realize I was not in the least ready. If they would have come at the time I thought they should have happened, I would not have gained anything. Indeed, I would have lost something.

Perhaps you know of someone or even have been present in the situation where a house has been sold, and then during the escrow period, the sale falls through. In many of these instances, I have employed the idea of "the blessing of delay" as an affirmation. It is not very long until a much better offer and property deal comes along, with more cash, better terms, or a more qualified buyer. What results is the best for all concerned. Perhaps the lesson that can be learned from the idea of "the blessing of delay" is patience. Quite simply this means that we must remain calm, steadfast, waiting out the working of the Law its own way and its own time.

Let us recall an old axiom made new: "God, please give me patience—and I want it right now, this minute." We need to learn and then remind ourselves frequently that everything happens at exactly the right time in exactly the right way—every time. God, I have learned, is never late; God's way is always on time. You cannot hurry up your good just as you cannot delay it. All is Good, and it appears at the right time. Realize this.

Even your problems happen at the exact, right moment. If you disagree, tell me when would you be ready for them? Interesting thought, don't you think? What if you took on the concept that your "problem" is your next lesson for growth?

"Whatever is, is," Buddha said (therein he defined the Truth). This marvelous idea is a great spiritual reminder that whatever is happening is right on time.

The word "delay," an interesting word to study, means to slacken, to loosen, to untie, to postpone, to alter, to detain, or keeping in one's possession. It also means to retard.

Now, apply these definitions to your so-called "delay." When faced with blockage, an obstacle that seems to be thwarting your good, remember it.

The Blessing of Delay

Could you loosen up? Could you slacken the tension in your body? Could you delay, postpone, defer your anger? Could you—would you—alter your reactions? Could you retard or slow down your usual normal reaction to this intangible thing called "delay?"

Let us examine another meaning for the word "delay." Why are you delaying the giving up of those things that impede your progress, that is, keeping whatever you are keeping in your mental possession, such as anger, apprehension (a form of fear) and anxiety?

I remember my last delay experience with an airline. A flight I was to take was postponed for one hour, then for another hour—then still another hour. It went on and on into the afternoon. I had a glorious opportunity to apply the principle of "the blessing of delay."

I worked on delaying my temper! I untied myself from the remarks and feelings of those around me and those traveling with me. It was a rather magnificent test of what I had come to believe about the "blessing of delay." This was a true life test! A test of whatever is, is!

Years prior to my metaphysical education, I would, in this particular instance of delayed air flight, have been the professional Italian-American I had been reared to be. I would have reacted in a totally opposite way from the manner in which I handled that particular situation of delay. You can imagine the drama I might have caused, with full orchestra, blaring trumpets, and crying strings, containing the sound and fury of two sopranos, a bass and tenor, and a very large chorus following me up.

Is there anyone who has not had the experience

49

of ordering an item or furnishing from a store, having been promised delivery on a certain date, and waited at home for what came to be a non-arrival? You called the store and their reply was to tell you that there was a mixup on the order. It would be delivered the following morning—and again, it did not arrive. What can you do about it? Is it worth the hassle, the anger, the emotion, the adrenalin, or the possibility of a heart attack to pursue it?

I remember a while back I decided to have a piece of furniture refinished. It took several months before it was in my home. Was there anything I could have done about it? Could I go over to the refinisher and shoot him? Or even argue with him? Of course not. So, I diverted my attention, saying, "The furniture is in my home at exactly the right time, and not one moment earlier!" It was there sooner than later, and it is beautiful, certainly worth waiting for without the grief.

How many of us have had a plumber promise us he would arrive at ten o'clock one morning? We sit looking at the clock until he finally shows himself at five o'clock. Or an auto repairman promises the car no later than Tuesday, and here it is Thursday. The last time you went by the repair shop you could swear it had not been moved from where you had placed it. What could you do? Absolutely nothing except relax, knowing that everything is in time, on time, every time. During the waiting, find something creative to do, something that can fulfill you—clean the closets, fix the picnic table, mend the fence, build a birdhouse, stitch a quilt, lower or raise those hems, read a biography of a successful person or an engrossing "trashy" novel. Make delay an opportunity to expand yourself in a long forgotten, when-I-have-some-time-on-my-hands-I'll-do-it task.

Now, delaying that seems to be imposed on you by other forces does not mean we need to become doormats. This doesn't mean we let other people take advantage of our time. Here, once more, I hear the Serenity Prayer and apply its wisdom to our situation: "I can't change them; I can only change my reaction to them. I can accept the things I cannot change, and pray for the courage to change the things I can change."

This does not in the least mean that we procrastinate or take a "slow-poke" attitude toward what we do, or what others are doing. It means we have to be realistic and not expect other people to behave as we want them to behave—to realize that other people might not work as fast, as well, as wonderfully as we do.

I am a person who is punctual. Rarely, if ever, am I late for an appointment, a dinner, or luncheon date. Never in my years in the ministry have I been late to church. There is always within me that song made famous by Stanley Holloway: "Get Me to the Church on Time."

Although I am punctual, how do I react when I deal with, or have an appointment with, someone who seems thoughtless to time? Or with someone who is notoriously, or even "fashionably," late? When someone is not on time for an appointment, I do not drum my fingers, or wonder where they are. I simply get busy doing something else.

Most often, when a person arrives late, I say, "I am SO glad you were late; I got so much work done!"

This has taught me to become most selective when it comes to choosing someone to work on the car, or do the new drapes, or refinish furniture. If the craftsperson or the mechanic does not satisfy you (or me) the first time, you just do not need to return to that person. And it is all right to calmly let them know why you are taking your business elsewhere.

I have read that it takes the little chick five hundred pecks to come out of its shell at birth. (No, I do not know who took time to count the pecks.) But it is reported that, if you try to help the little chick be born, to come out of its shell, if you try to help it along, it will die. It must birth its own way, in its own time. That means to me that there is an intelligence within that little chick that knows the exact time it must come forth. We can deduce from that example that if we want an idea to birth, there is the exact time or exposure that that idea needs in order to come into being—to be made manifest. So, in the realm of God, there is no haste. In the God-Mind there is no delay.

Do you know the wonderful story about the caterpillar crawling up the trunk of a tree? A bird watches the caterpillar making its slow ascent. Sarcastically, the bird says, "Why are you coming up here? There are no peaches on this tree."

The caterpillar, just lumbering along, says in a most assured manner, "There will be by the time I get there."

Everything is on time, every time. Even peaches.

Often we in metaphysics say our affirmations, and our declarations of the achievement is stated as NOW! We shout to the Universe, "My healing is now!" Then we look at ourselves, still lying sick in bed.

We shout to the Universe, "I have my abundance NOW!" Then we look at our checkbook. There seems to be something saying, "Are you kidding? Look at this!"

We realize that there is a creative process that is involved in the healing of the physical, mental, or the financial. We know there is the creative process and it does involve time. We know that Time itself is a strange, nebulous thing. Can we accept this fact?

Who on this planet has ever placed a tomato plant in the garden and then an hour later gone to the yard and picked a tomato? When a baby is conceived, there is a time process for the total development of the baby. The child's full formation is not instantaneous. We plant a seed and we await its growth. There is something between the seed and the plant that we have absolutely nothing to do with. So we turn it over to that Great Intelligence, that Divine Process of evolution, of unfoldment. We turn it to the Law of Mind, and the fulfillment of the event is according to the Universal Law.

Last year, a young lady of our church family was "large with child." She confided that, according to her doctor, the baby was late. He had predicted, as a function of his medical practice, the baby's birth for a particular date. That day had passed, and she was three weeks past due.

I assured her of the idea of delay, that God is never late, always on time, in time, every time. I assured her that babies are born, not to a doctor's calendar, but delivered according to God's calendar, and the agreement of the baby person.

And it was!

There is a Divine reason for the baby to be born "late." The baby, following its Divine Plan, has something to say about when it is to be born. I am of the belief that babies choose their time. The Divine Selector of the right time is within that baby's Mind-Spirit. It knows when the complete formation of that creation of God is ready to leave its warm, safe place to enter the world to fulfill itself as a human being.

Whether it is a baby being born, or whether we are designing a home, a dress, a suit, or garden, it takes that thing called Time to get it off the paper into actual form.

A few years ago, I experienced a classic example of this. There was in our church a fine young man who was devoted to the teaching, Science of Mind. He was a licensed practitioner in our church—and devout in his belief.

Then, he had an accident; he broke his foot and was unable to walk except with the aid of crutches. His cast was placed from the foot to the hip. His doctor had told him that it would take approximately three to four months before the foot would heal and his cast could be removed.

One day, he said to me that, since he was a practitioner, and since he was a believer in instantaneous healing, and since he performed his prayer treatments sincerely, including daily affirmations, he was going to remove that cast himself, at that moment. He told me, if he could not do that right then, that he was certain he was not an effective practitioner and he could not continue with his religious science studies.

He took up some tools then, and he began to remove pieces of the cast. I pleaded with him to stop. I reminded him that there was a time process involved in healing and, in attempting to hurry it, could be quite dangerous to his whole healing. I reminded him of the five hundred pecks of the chicken. He ignored my attempt to rationalize as he kept picking away at the plaster cast.

This young man had assisted in the renovation of our church sanctuary. I suddenly recalled the time when we had ordered draperies for the window behind the lectern. I said to this young man, "My friend, remember when we ordered those draperies for the church window?" (They were to arrive from Sweden.) "I kept asking you over and over when, When, WHEN will they arrive? And you kept saying to me, 'It takes time, Dr. Tom. It takes time!' Be patient!" (And it did take time— about three months for those draperies to arrive in Palm Desert.)

The man stopped his picking away at the cast. He looked at me for a moment, then put down his tool. Suddenly he realized from that experience, whether it's drapes arriving or the manifestation of his own healing, the creative process of most everything takes time. "There is a time for all things, a time for all seasons, each to its own," the saying goes.

Let everything unfold easily and divinely. What we call "delay" could be called a creative process of the Universe. It says, "NOW is the time!" Not your time, not the calendar's time, not the time of the clock. But that timelessness of all the ages.

There are some things that do seem to arrive instantly, and their permanent place with us is according to our beliefs. There are things that we pray for and treat for—the things that are already here. However, we need to await our total, unconditional belief in their presence before they are manifested, before they are in front of us or part of our life experience. All things are for our good and our growth. Everything we can perceive has its rhythm of experiencing. We need to know those things that can only come to us in steps—in the rhythm of their own consciousness. Also, we need to recognize that those materials and feelings that seem to appear to us immediately have, in essence, been on their own pathway to us before their actual appearance.

I know it. And so, too, do you know it!

Remember, "In every delay, there is a blessing on its way."

5

Someday Isle

I have done a good deal of traveling in my life. I've had the good fortune to visit many parts of this glorious planet. Unfortunately, however, there is one place that I have visited that I really could have done without. It is one of those places that we all have journeyed to, and I say that we ought to have just stayed home!

This particular place is very elusive. People talk about it a great deal, yet the many who talk of it never quite get there. It is not at all exclusive—it is visited and thought about by millions of people.

There are no travel brochures for this place. Travel agents cannot book you into that spot. You can't take pictures or buy postcards of this special place.

By this time you may think, what is he talking about—where is he talking about?

I speak here of that mythical island that is not on any map; nor is it included in any travel or geography book. It is a place I call "Someday Isle."

Have you ever heard of that "island paradise," so called? Have you ever talked about that favorite spot of the stars and the masses?

Yes, most of us have, and our looking to that "paradisc" is cxactly what keeps us from enjoying the "mainland." We talk about it so much that we give up our place in the mainstream of Life. We easily drift off into that "never-never" land, Someday Isle.

If you have not quite figured it all out, then listen to your friends; listen closely to yourself, and you will hear, "Someday, I'll be happy." "Someday I'll meet the right person." "Someday my ship will come in and I'll be rich." "Someday I'll go on a diet." And the list goes on. "Someday I'll write that book." "Someday I'll compose that song, paint that picture, clean out the garage...someday I'll leave him once and for all." "Someday I'll make that call, write that letter of forgiveness." "Someday I will...."

We could go on with, "Someday I'll give up the booze, the cigarettes, the drugs, the Past, and 'twinkies,' not necessarily in that order." Or, "Someday, somewhere, over a rainbow, happy little bluebirds fly; if happy little bluebirds fly across the rainbow, why can't I?"

Good question!

The best way to get your life off the ground is to stop and curtail that "Someday, I'll..." kind of consciousness. (Someday I may even change my mind.) Otherwise, if we do not cease this kind of thought, we will surely make that someday place a sort of Nirvana. Perhaps it has already reached that point for some. Such someday talk becomes our Shangri-La. It ends up being the proverbial carrot in front of the donkey's nose—that which we never quite seem to reach.

Many of us are always just a little step behind our good, just a tad behind our joy, just a snort behind our happiness. Many of us seem always on the verge of something glorious, but something or someone always holds us back.

The only thing that holds us back is an idea— one single thought. God doesn't know we cannot do something. We do, however. And that which we need to eliminate from our consciousness is the idea that we cannot do something. All we need to know about any problem we may have—including this going off to Someday Island—is, in this case, an equal and opposite idea or thought.

Someday Isle

My mail ministry has expanded greatly over the past few years. I found that I had a drawer filled with letters. "Someday, I'll answer those letters," I said. The drawer became so filled with letters from far and near that I could barely open it.

The answer, the idea that I needed was to write on my envelopes the addresses of the people who had written me and then to actually put stamps on them. I would stack them and then one by one, the letters would be answered. This eliminated the "someday-I'll-answer-those-letters" stage of procrastination.

(Who would want to waste or leave idle an envelope with a twenty-five-cent stamp on it?)

Sometimes the Someday-I'll type of thinking becomes more attractive than actually doing it. Often the effort we spend on the procrastination is greater than the effort it would take to perform the task. The "someday-I'll-clean-out-the-garage" example is one we are familiar with. The debris piles up so much it becomes a hardship when you finally get around to cleaning and straightening it out. We have to consider leaving Someday Isle, and moving into the action that is before us today.

I remember well my first trip to Europe in the summer of 1958. Until that time, I had said many times over (it would seem thousands of times), "Someday I'll go to Europe." Then someone actually called my bluff one day, saying, "You talk but you don't do. I doubt if you'll ever get to Europe."

I was furious. "I'll show you!" I said.

I called the airline and made the reservations. Since I had done that, I had to obtain a passport;

since I had done that, I had to start putting money aside for the trip.

The next thing I knew I was stepping off the plane in Copenhagen. But that happened only after I took some action. I stopped talking about what I was going to do and began to do it.

"Be doers of the word," the Bible tells us.

When I was in the bar business (not the legal bar, the liquid bar), nightly I heard people who sat on the stools talking endless hours about what they were going to do or what they wished they had done.

They were talkers, not doers. The moral of the story is: If we keep sitting around waiting for our ship to come in, it just may be unwelcome when it arrives.

I recall seeing a greeting card once that said something like, "Just my luck, when my ship comes in, I'll probably be at the airport." No ship comes in unless you start that action by sending it out from the pier. If you do not start a journey, you will never arrive at your destination.

In the gospel of Luke it is written that Jesus said, "All that I have is thine!" Notice it does not say, "Someday I'll give you what is yours!" What this says, in essence, is that this is the Kingdom that I am giving you now. You and I already have it. Now what are you and I going to do with it?

The author of the Twenty-third Psalm writes, "The Lord is my Shepherd...." That "is" means now! It does not imply that "Someday, I will be your shepherd." So, don't use yesterday or tomorrow as a yardstick for what you can do today.

I repeat, if you do not start a trip, you will never arrive anywhere. Whether it is a trip, a relationship, a painting, or a song, it must have a beginning. Make last night the last night you complain about Life and not being happy. Remember that happiness comes in "cans," not in "can'ts."

Don't mortgage your future by declaring how hopeless "things" are today. Stop awfulizing. "Isn't it awful?" is a waste of precious time. When we speak of times, precious or otherwise, we try to keep up with the times. Keeping up with the times does not mean, in my opinion, wearing wide or thin ties, or high or low hems, spiked or flat heels. Keeping up with the times means, "How are we updating our thinking?" "How are we improving our reactions, our attitudes, our beliefs—have we changed one belief lately?"

Emerson said, "If you believe today what you believed yesterday, you are not growing."

Today, in this moment of time, let us sing, "Now is the hour," and wave farewell to that mythical island, that isle of someday. That isle of "pretty soon," that isle of "it-won't-be-long-now." Let us avoid the isle of "It's right around the corner."

There is not a farmer who has ever lived who has ever plowed a field by turning it over only in his mind. There is no successful engineer who has not seen his plans get off the drawing board. Procrastination is the fertilizer that makes difficulties grow.

How many days have we spent in the prison of self-induced bondage by saying to ourselves, "Someday I'll write that letter of apology." "Someday I'll run into her, and we'll straighten it out then."

Putting off doing something about *something* makes the doing of something harder to do. Or haven't you noticed? The fence you put up or the wall you build just gets higher and higher to climb.

The verse of Psalm 118:24 is a good reminder of this. "This is the day which the Lord hath made; Let us rejoice and be glad in it." We can no longer push our good away from us, when we know that it is only a new thought or a new idea that could tear that wall down—that could release us from the fear of tomorrow and, more especially, the load of yesterday.

Let us turn yesterday into "Yes, today!"

Say it. "Yes, today is the day I arrange to start those classes." "Yes, today I begin to write that book." "Yes, today I begin to paint that picture."

Not tomorrow! Today!

"Yes, today is the day that I let go of my pain, my misery, my sorry story." "I live this moment, free." "I do not regret the past moments, nor do I fear the future ones."

We hear the cries, "When the kids grow up; when the car is paid off; when I get out of college...." Just as with my first trip to Europe, just as I began my first book, just as I knew I had to leave the bar business and get into the ministry, I knew that I had to leave Someday Isle. And I had to know I would not return again! Too many losers live on Someday Isle; too many underachievers have settled there for the duration.

I grew up in a "Someday I'll" family. My father hated his work, and he constantly talked of his "Someday I'll retire, and then I will really be living." He was a hard worker; he provided well for his family. But his "Someday I'll" kind of thinking eventually caught up with him. He passed on shortly after his retirement. He never left Someday Isle for that place called "reality."

64

I speak from experience, not from theory. I believe that today is the day that you could do it. Do whatever it is that fulfills your want, your wish, or your dream. Making plans and setting goals are great. Wonderful. But one day the idea, as the step of a plan, must begin.

I like what Picasso said when he was asked to name his favorite painting from all of his work. "My next one," he responded. He knew he couldn't stop only to rest upon the laurels of yesterday. He knew that the trick to painting, either as art or enjoyment, was to keep painting—that this alone was the ultimate reward.

We need to stop our living by proxy. We need to stop living via television sit-coms or soap operas. Let us enjoy them, but let us acknowledge that they are produced on Someday Isle. Oftentimes sitting in our living room we watch the people on television who are people we would not invite into our own living room. But to me, watching them in their roles on our screens is almost the same thing as having them sit across the room from us.

I read Vincent Van Gogh was a person who continually berated his own talent and squelched his ability to be happy. He made a statement that truly "shot him down" years before he actually shot himself: "It is absolutely certain that I shall never do anything important; here and there, some of my work might last a while."

His painting *Irises* sold for 53.9 million dollars recently. Because of this work and others like it, he is ranked as being among the world's most acclaimed artists. Yet, he said, "I am a nonentity who has no place in society, and I never will have." This vein of degradation brings me to Whittier who wrote, "For all sad words of tongue and pen, the saddest are these: 'It might have been.' "

Let me give you another of Costa's Laws for Life: Don't be a Van Gogh; do not degrade yourself. Don't be like my father or countless others who are going to be happy at some future day at some other place. Dream your dream, but when you wake up make it become your truth.

I love what performer Dolly Parton once said: "I have never quit trying, and I have never tried quitting." Marvelous!

Back in 1973, I telephoned my parents in western Pennsylvania to tell them I was going to quit bartending. "I'm going into the ministry," I said with joy in my heart and voice.

My father pleaded with me to stay where I was. "You don't know what the ministry holds for you," he said. "Stay with what you know. You'll be giving up your retirement pension."

First of all, my pension would have amounted to fifty dollars a month, which would not have purchased sufficient food for my dogs! Secondly, I realized that my father was speaking from his own feelings of limitation. Countless thousands of men and women like him stay with what they know. They never take a risk, a chance to grow, to attempt something. They stay on Someday Isle and live vicariously through travel brochures and television shows. The dreams stay under their pillows never to see the daylight of risk and reality.

In 1973, at age fifty-one, I had to leave that comfort zone and give it a go. Little did I know that it would eventually turn out to be a ministry of over a thousand people and that I would not only become successful, but I would be helping so many others into getting themselves off Someday Isle—to live, instead of merely existing.

My parents never lived to see our church building and the crowds coming to hear me each Sunday. However, I am certain that wherever they are, they know, I know, and God knows about my work today.

I realize that, as I changed my thinking and left that isle of isolation and got into the action of my thinking, doing, being, and having, that I was impelled, compelled, and propelled to teach others that they, too, can accomplish the same thing— their fulfillment. Isn't that a take-off of what Jesus said when he said, "You, too, can do greater works than I if you but believe."

Surely we know now that metaphysically we cannot do greater works if we hold onto our old ideas. My parents, who were poor—I was raised during the Great Depression—held onto ideas of poverty and limitation their whole lives. This was their true lifestyle in that time frame.

As my ministry grew, my lifestyle changed. I would stay in nicer hotels in the better parts of the cities I visited; I became used to leaving my shoes outside the hotel room door to have them polished in the morning (rather than being swiped).

One day as I was leaving a very expensive hotel, I realized I had always taken the soap, the shampoo, conditioner, and toner from the little basket in the bathroom. I took these home, but I never used them.

I could not understand at the moment of realization why I did this. One day, in meditation, I flashed back to the time when we were poor and my mother wasted absolutely nothing. She would take slivers of soap and work them together to make little pieces of soap into bigger pieces of soap.

I recognized suddenly that because of this I had been doing something automatically for years. Until that moment of realization I never knew why I took soap from hotel bathrooms.

I can afford a cake of soap. I can afford the soap I like. Now when I travel I take my favorite soap, my favorite toner, or whatever is necessary. I was healed of an impulsive habit instantly. As Phineas Quimby declared, "The explanation is the cure!"

Not unlike the matter of my first tuxedo. Within this ministry, there are many occasions when I must wear a tuxedo. In the past I invariably ended up with a white sport coat, black trousers, and a black tie, which I substituted for my "tux."

Not too long ago, I was invited to give the invocation at the swankiest affair of the year in Palm Desert—I knew I had to get a tux. I kept resisting, and I kept being thwarted from shopping for one. In my meditation period I pondered the idea: what is my resistance? Suddenly, I flashed again to my father. He hated rich people! He would often say how hard he worked in his life and that the rich never worked a day in their lives. He believed that.

Subjectively, very subtly, I had assumed his belief of equating a tuxedo with wealth! As soon as that came into my mind, realizing my resistance from this past belief of another person, I was again healed of a belief that I had set on "automatic." Until that realization I never knew why I did not own a tux.

What I had done was come off the "someday-I'll-wear-a-tux" thinking (for inside myself I really yearned to own and wear one). This knowledge was an important step in my cutting the umbilical cord from my family and gaining new beliefs about myself. The umbilical cord to our parents' beliefs is not just a thread. It is a huge rope, with many layers and levels. It seems all too often that we keep cutting, and cutting. Can we ever quite break through, break clear, break free?

Yes. When we recognize that a belief that limits us belongs to someone else, we can find the power within ourselves to change it. Every time we cut into, and cut away from, our old beliefs, we are happier, we are healthier, we are wealthier. We are another step farther away from Someday Isle.

The following text, a wise writing by Portia Nelson, is the story of my life; perhaps others can relate to it.

Autobiography in Five Short Chapters
by
Portia Nelson

I

I walk down the street.
   There is a deep hole in the sidewalk.
I fall in
I am lost...I am helpless,
   It isn't my fault.
It takes forever to find a way out.

II

I walk down the same street.
   There is a deep hole in the sidewalk.
   I pretend I don't see it.
   I fall in again.

I can't believe I am in the same place,
　　but, it isn't my fault.
It still takes a long time to get out.

III
I walk down the same street.
　　There is a deep hole in the sidewalk.
　　I see it is there.
　　I still fall in...it's a habit,
　　　　my eyes are open.
　　I know where I am.
　　It is my fault.
　　I get out immediately.

IV
I walk down the same street.
　　There is a deep hole in the sidewalk.
　　I walk around it.

V
I walk down another street.

6

Making the Unbearable Bearable

There are very few persons who have lived, or will ever live, who at some time in life will be without what seems an unbearable situation. It may be a short-lived event or condition, or it could be a long period calling upon the man or woman to utilize the principles of endurance.

Certainly, there is the unbearable moment for a child whose toy is broken or whose pet is gravely ill. Or it seems that the end of the world has come for a young person who is not selected as a high-school cheerleader. To a person who has the "perfect" job, there is the unbearable time when it is taken from him.

Unbearable seems the moment when a Life partner dies. The list is endless as we spend time thinking about unbearable situations.

In retrospect, we view those times when we cried out to the Universe, "Why me? Why now? Why not someone else, God? I've been a good person; I've never harmed anyone. Why did this unbearable situation drop in my lap?"

Can you relate to any of these heart-rending questions? I certainly can.

(With cameras grinding and lights flashing!)

How many of us have had what can be defined in a moment as an insurmountable challenge—a problem so great that we are at the point of locating the nearest towel and throwing it in. Too often we raise the white flag of surrender, move to our respective corners to stay there for the remainder of our lives, never wanting to come out again to fight the battle. Some folks call behavior like this "playing it safe." I call it surrender.

At times you scream from within, "If one more thing happens, I will just flip!"

And it does—and sometimes you do!

What do you find yourself doing? You might do as I have done in many instances. Laugh—yes, actually laugh—at how Life has piled up against me all at once.

"The nicest thing about the future is that it comes one day at a time," John Foster Dulles once said. So I know, and you ought to know, that we can handle all the problems Life has to give us.

These reactions of laughter tell me that there is an "easy does it" side to all lives that helps us make the unbearable bearable. Some of us have to learn what laughter is, how to produce it, how to allow it to come up from inside us, and how to define it as "the best medicine" for our bodies and minds.

For years, I've had a friend named Gil. Years ago, while he was working on his car, his hand slipped and the screwdriver he was using caused him the loss of sight in his right eye. Gil quickly accepted what happened to him and used the situation as an opportunity.

Although he had made his choice, his family could not accept the fact that he had the use of only one eye. They spoke of the accident and its result in whispers—never talking about it when he was around. They more or less pretended that it had not happened. His friends, including me, also did not discuss it in front of or with him. Because of this, Gil wanted to do something so that his unbearable situation would be bearable to his family and friends. He came up with an idea: get a false eye. This, however, did not seem to help the situation. When he looked in a certain direction, the false eye stayed in place—staring straight ahead. Then people would stare back. (Often a person would want to glance back over their shoulder to see just what the eye was looking at!) "How can I help my family and my friends accept what I have already accepted?" Gil asked himself.

Gil's glorious sense of humor had him order some new false eyes. On one false eye he had painted a turkey—to wear during the Thanksgiving holiday. He had another eye painted with a Christmas tree, which he donned for the Yuletide season. Another eye was prepared for Independence Day. His Fourth of July eye had a firecracker on it. Still another was painted with an Easter lily.

The reaction of family and friends, of course, was laughter. Laughter is always based upon the unexpected. Certainly these various painted eyes were the last thing people expected to see. What Gil did with his humorous idea was to bring into this unbearable situation comic relief.

Occasionally, at a party in his home, Gil would place an eye, a clean one, at the bottom of the punch bowl—until his wife would scream at him, "Get that thing out of there!"

There is a great difference between acceptance for what has happened to us and total resignation. Looking at the bright side of Life is one of the best antidotes for misery, pain, and anxiety. If one resigns himself to the Fates, he gives up his control of his life experience. He gives up the lessons of Life.

Dr. Lee S. Berk, an assistant research professor of pathology at Loma Linda Hospital in California, has been studying the healing properties of laughter. At this highly respected medical center, they now conduct a humor therapy program, bending the rules considerably about what heals disease and disharmony in the body.

Dr. Berk predicts that laughter-inducing comedy may become an integral part of medical care in years to come. Berk maintains that if you have a "blithe spirit" and laugh a lot, beneficial physical changes can be induced.

Laughter is, as it has been written, the medicine of the soul. "A merry heart doeth good like a medicine. But a broken spirit dryeth the bones." (Proverbs 17:22)

Many doctors, such as Dr. Berk, are finding that people with a good sense of humor have better survival and recovery rates than people who take everything seriously, seldom laughing. Dr. William Fry, a Stanford University psychiatrist has said, "Adults laugh an average of about fifteen times a day, compared with normal healthy children who laugh four hundred times daily." Dr. Berk has added that "Somewhere between childhood and adulthood we lose three hundred and eighty-five laughs a day."

Now, this does not mean that when you are in the divorce court, when you are in the hospital with an intravenous tube in your arm and tubes up your nose, dressed in a full-length plaster cast, that you necessarily need to read a comic book, laughing hysterically. But laughter can be an important part of your physical and spiritual healing. Therefore, we have to be very serious about not being so serious.

This very idea was brought up during a seminar when Dr. Gerald Jampolsky said, "Let go, let God, and lighten up!"

I am confident many students of self-healing

practices have read or heard of Dr. Norman Cousins and his magnificent book, *The Anatomy of an Illness*.

"A hospital is no place for a sick person," he wrote. So, while still experiencing his pain, he signed himself out of the hospital, went home, rented Laurel and Hardy and Charlie Chaplin movies, and literally laughed himself to health. Dr. Cousins found that ten minutes of good laughter gave him two hours of pain-free sleep.

Isn't this why we often refer to a laugh as a "hearty laugh?" Dr. Cousins calls laughter "internal jogging."

Hippocrates, the father of medicine, refers to the "humors" of the body—meaning the fluids. Balancing our humors with laughter helps us take our focus off the immediate problem, the insurmountable and the unbearable, so that the healing Presence of God, as the healing essence, can do miraculous things without our specification, direction, or supervision.

The message here is to laugh at and with yourself more than you do. Look seriously at that factor that caused you to lose those three hundred and eighty-five laughs a day. "Laugh and the world laughs with you; cry and you cry alone," is the old adage. Laugh and your body will respond divinely and magnificently. It shakes the cells and the muscles. The blood flows at an increased pace. Then the body comes to be at ease with itself instead of being in a state of dis-ease.

Sometimes I truly laugh at myself when I think of what my life used to be like. At one time I had so many unbearable problems that, if anything else terrible had happened to me, it would have taken quite a while before I could have gotten around to worrying about it. I was at least two weeks behind in my worrying!!!

Not anymore.

I came to realize at a point in my life that a problem not worth praying about really was not worthy of worrying about. It was Dr. Catherine Ponder who hit me over the head with "If you pray, don't worry. If you worry, don't waste your time on prayer."

We have to go within ourselves. We need to look within to the center of our self, searching within to that core to find out what can cause us to bear up to the unbearable. If we do not go within, we go without—we go without the answer, the healing, and the wholeness of our health.

One of the best ways to start is to learn to re-lease the three Rs and I don't mean Readin', 'Riting, and 'Rithmetic. Here, I mean the three Rs as Resentment, Regret, and Righteousness.

The word resentment comes from the French word *resentir*, meaning to re-feel. So when we resent something, or someone, we are RE-FEELING the incident, the pain, the memory, although we may be totally unaware of this.

This leads us to regret. What good is regret? Life is like toothpaste: Once it is out of the tube, you can't get it back in.

Then comes Righteousness. Oh, how many times have we sacrificed our sanity and peace of mind in order to be right! It's a high price to pay. "After all, right is right." Sound familiar?

Work on those three Rs, then watch your life improve. Watch for more happiness and joy to come into your life. And remember: Judgment, I have found, is the mud that we sling at our own happiness.

Learn to be THROUGH with a situation once you have gone *through* it. I love to remind people of my special paraphrase of the Twenty-Third Psalm. "Yea, though you walk THROUGH the valley of the shadow of death, you don't have to build a house there." The active word here is "through."

I remind myself often of a lady I was once counseling who said to me, "Dr. Tom, I am going through hell!"

"Don't stop!" I said to her.

"You really don't know what I'm going through," I have so often heard.

Right! So keep going, I say. Going through something means there is action taking place.

If you are still discussing your problem with eighty-seven of your most intimate friends or if you are still cussing the problem out, you are obviously not through with it.

(And count your blessings if you still have your eighty-seven friends listening to you.)

There is an old saying that "Iron must go through fire to become steel." Personally, I can see this is true. All of the unbearable situations I have moved THROUGH have truly made me stronger and more firm in my belief that it is not important what happens to me, but only how I handle what is happening to me.

(If you choose, read again the last sentence and substitute "you" in place of "me" and "I.")

79

Life is not unlike painting a picture. Judge Thomas Troward has said, "You can't see the picture if you are still in the frame." At times you need to stand back from the canvas and look at it, to see what is happening—to see the balance or imbalance.

I read about Beverly Sills, the opera singer, who gave up her career while it was still at its peak in order to take over the management of the New York City Opera Company. The story goes that Ms. Sills wears a gold chain and medallion around her neck on which are four gold letters: I.D.T.A.

It is said she was so weary of answering the question as to why she gave up her singing career to manage the opera company that she would point to the letters on the medallion to explain, "I DID THAT ALREADY."

How well I relate to that statement! I am confident every reader can also relate to it. I have done enough misery to last me an eternity—I.D.T.A.—I Did That Already.

I have done enough resentment and enough regret in my life that I just don't want to do *that* anymore. I DID THAT ALREADY. This is a glorious idea, realizing that we do not have to go through that valley, through that hell, through that pain again and again simply because we did all that before. We do have the power of choice to NOT do those things again.

"Pure, unadulterated insanity is doing the same thing over and over and expecting things to be different," says my good friend, Dr. Peggy Bassett.

Realizing you don't have to repeat the same experiences unless you choose to is one of the greatest, most effective ways of making the unbearable bearable.

The word "bear," which is within the word "unbearable" is interesting to contemplate. It can mean "to be productive," or it can mean "to yield." For example, women can bear children; the trees bear fruit. Or it can mean "to endure, to suffer, to tolerate," or even to bear a cross. Our choice is to help make the unbearable situation produce or yield a lesson from within it. Then we can make our cross to bear a serendipitous event in our lives. You will find the gift in the lesson, be it patience, be it tolerance, be it kindness.

Speaking of crosses, I noticed that there is never one cross for two persons to bear; it is always a cross made for one. This means to me that when we bear our cross, it is singular, self-created, self-sustained, and self-maintained.

It is written in the Bible that Jesus bore his cross for three hours then he put it down. Similarly, we have to lay our crosses down in order to look at the situation from a different perspective—that is, creating the inner ability to resurrect ourselves from our own self-inflicted punishment.

Forgiveness is a most effective way to make many unbearable situations tolerable. Forgiveness is a marvelous way to come down from your cross. The word "forgiveness" comes from an Aramaic word which means "to untie." So when we forgive ourselves or the other person, or simply let go, we are mentally and emotionally untying ourselves from that situation, from that person, or from that painful memory.

Too, age does not seem to have too much affect on life's doling out the unbearable. I spoke once at a youth-group rally where there were about one hundred and fifty young people present. I mentioned the unbearable moments in one's life, and the general consensus was that, when someone leaves you or rejects you when you are sixteen, it is just as unbearable as when someone leaves you or rejects you at the age of forty. I was surprised how many young people came to me after the talk and told me they could relate to what I had said, although there was an age gap of about fifty years. Many who were fourteen and fifteen had felt that feeling of total despair and hopelessness—to the point of contemplating suicide. I shared with them that when I was twenty-one I tried suicide because I had nothing to live for, or so I thought. How sad it would have been had I succeeded in that act.

(Sad, of course, for so many people whose lives would not have been so enriched by my presence! And I would have missed so much drama—and more love than drama.)

An unbearable moment can be a fleeting thing, or it can fester for a long period—to the depths of our being. However, it is important that we confront the "thing." We must know that, no matter what, we can make it through the night, the day, or the hour of our despair.

This takes us back to that which was mentioned earlier: the difference between acceptance and resignation. Many people who have horrendous things happen to them pick themselves up, dust themselves off, and they *do* start all over again, as my friend Gil did.

I think of Mrs. Rose Kennedy, whose life has been touched so many times with tragedy. Besides this great lady, there are countless thousands of people who have accepted whatever has happened to them and then moved on with their lives.

Conversely, there are also countless thousands of people who have simply resigned themselves to their events, like an old man who wants to talk of nothing but his gall-bladder operation (that took place sixteen years earlier). They refuse to start up again whether it be financially, emotionally, or mentally. That catastrophe becomes the focal point of their lives not only for a week, a month, but an entire lifetime! No one in earshot will ever hear of anything else but "The time that...."

My mind flashes to the first three words in Dr. Scott Peck's book, *The Road Less Traveled*. He opens with the comment "Life is difficult." I cringed when I first opened the book and read that sentence. How can anyone start a book like that—especially when you are reading it to obtain some sort of spiritual and emotional assistance! But those three words surely grab your attention. Those words start your thinking processes. Those words make you sit up and take notice of the truth within the statement.

(That which is, is!)

No. Life is not easy.

However, accepting the idea that life is difficult doesn't mean that you give up, throw in the towel, or resign yourself to the situation. It can mean that you accept what has happened and you brace yourself and start anew from there. You just begin from right where you are!

Remember, your problems always arrive on time. Of course they do—for if it was your choice, when would you be ready for them?

Life! You Wanna Make Something of It?

What does it mean if you are fired from a job?

(I dislike the word "fired" used this way—it sounds as if you are being shot from a cannon. Here, I prefer the word "released.")

When released from a job, it is time to go within yourself, not to ask "Why," but to ask where to go next. What have you gained from what has happened? Emotionally, what have you learned about yourself from this experience?

This can also mean that when someone moves out of your experience, as Emerson said: "When an angel walks out of your life, there's an archangel ready to walk in."

That statement has assisted me so much when there was suddenly a great void in my life. It is said, "Nature abhors a vacuum." I have found this to be very true. So we have to be realistic and realize that things come into your life to go out of your life; people come into your life only to one day move out of it; money comes into your daily experience to pass out of your experience. Has any of it—of Life—ever stayed right with you? I have mentioned this idea earlier that things move in and out of Life, such as cars, clothes, books, houses, friends, thoughts, sunny days, rainy days, and the seasons. Nothing stays around forever—except the Universe, that ever-changing intangible thing. And all happens in the Divine Right Order.

So the unbearable means that there is a change happening in your life. We can learn to accept change. Simply, accept you cannot change that thing called "change." You cannot fight it, either. I repeat what Leo Tolstoy once said: "Everyone wants the world to change but nobody wants to change."

We want the improvement without any change whatsoever.

That, my friends, is impossible.

When there is an unbearable situation, it never stays unbearable; there is that spiritual and mental bounce-back quality. "Homeostasis," I call it. As water seeks its own level eventually everything moves back to "normal."

(And if you try to define "normal," you can write your own book.)

When these things happen to us, we can test ourselves and see how flexible we are, to see what message within this text really works for us.

We can learn from those so-called unbearable moments in our lives. Our life events must become our teachers. If we do not allow them to be our teachers, then they are indeed our mistakes. Churning is learning. So when Life is in a turmoil, when the worst of the worst is happening, it is the time to look for the opportunities or the gift being presented to us by these events.

The Principle of Life is calling upon the source of your spirit, your true self, to listen to the voice within that says, "All is well, I am safe. I am a part of all that is, and all that is, is good."

I choose to call the good God. You may call it whatever you like. It *is* there. It is there for you, awaiting your call—to support you, to care for you.

This is the time to experiment with these ideas and to put them into action. When you finish this chapter, read it over again. Find a truth for yourself in the statements.

Most of us believe we learn through suffering—
that we learn through the "hard knocks" of Life.
Because we believe this, it becomes our reality—
"Hard Knocks."

"Hard knocks" are really opportunities for us to
grow. They are opportunities pounding down our
door and they can lead us to a great life through
correcting our thinking and our mental patterns.

There seems to be a large gathering of people in
this world who have had, or are having, the so-
called "unbearable situations." It may be gratifying
to all of them to know that others have been where
they are.

I believe that many persons who are reading
these ideas have shifted in their seats or taken a new
breath, or found a sense of relief, realizing that they
are not alone in an unbearable situation. If you desire to hold on to the event, however, you will come
into aloneness that affects your health—and your
spirit.

I believe, through experience, and through the
practice of affirming life experiences, that it is quite
probable you can be happy. You can resume your
life when you create the bearable from the unbearable experience.

7

What Really is Sacred?

When we emerge from an orthodox religion and move into the non-denominational New Age or New Thought philosophy, we find we need to forego a great deal of traditional ceremony and ritual. It is interesting to observe people taking up the informal aspects of a Sunday New Age service wherein "the word" is the primary focus over "the worship." If there is a worship to the New Thought teaching, it begins with the Self and the God within that Self. We are concerned with the spirit and the mind of the individual. It is our individual mind and spirit that is the Image of Spirit, which is God. And it is the spirit that extends itself to create our individual spirit. So, then, God-Spirit is within each of us.

In the first part of my life, as a Roman Catholic, my family practiced many sacred rites, paying homage and revering sacred people, places, and things in their worship. I am confident the same aspects of religious practice held true for those who were raised in the several Protestant denominations in the National Council of Churches.

It is noteworthy that my Italian-American family, which is still very Catholic, seems to revere Rome, the Vatican, and St. Peter's Cathedral more than Jerusalem—the city where the rabbi Jesus taught. I am the only person in our family who has ever been to Israel, although many in my family have made pilgrimages to Rome, the Vatican City.

Of course, although it may turn out to be humorous, I say that when I was younger I thought the gospel writers, Mark, Matthew, John and Luke were Italian! I was stunned at the moment I found they were not.

Dr. Rocco Errico once said that the painting of *The Last Supper* is a marvelous picture of twelve nice Italian men, because the men in the painting, who came from what is termed the ancient Holy Land, could not have appeared or dressed as they are portrayed in Leonardo's painting. There you have it again—a famous and sacred painting by an Italian who had probably never been to Jerusalem either!

Let us examine what we consider sacred. I was amazed as I researched those things considered sacred by certain peoples in various parts of the world. Some people have sacred weeds, sacred bark (that of the tree, not the sound from the family pet), sacred beans, and sacred mushrooms. Other folks honor sacred shirts, thread, beetles—even sacred rocks. In some places it's books, cows, even sacred ears! Or figs, fish, girdles, sacred iris, or lotus, or cord, or age, ape, or baboon! It's remarkable!

When you look at the list and include on it the many other sacred things that I, perhaps, did not find in my research, there does seem very little left out on the list of things people consider sacred. Except, of course, spaghetti—which, in my book, is most sacred!

"Sacred," the word, means to "set apart, to dedicate, to devote, to make holy, whole, to make hallowed." Now this kind of sacredness makes sense to me. But for someone to take a bean or a weed, or any of the other items on our list, and revere them is to revere something that is outside of the Self.

Many people revere the pulpit from which ministers, priests, and rabbis speak. Some consider my lectern a sacred place. In our church, on membership Sunday, we call the people to the podium to be acknowledged. Some ask not to be called forth because they feel uncomfortable about being in that "sacred" place. A few have said they felt as if they were trespassing where they ought not be.

There are people who feel there is more God on the podium where I speak the word than in the sanctuary where they sit.

Not so. In our philosophy and teaching, while it is named Religious Science because we study many religious and spiritual forms and principles that are, in reality, Universal Laws, the podium is simply a platform that elevates the speaker in order that he may be seen while he is speaking. And that which has been called the "sanctuary" is actually the auditorium. I believe it is as sacred out in the room, the sanctuary, or auditorium, as it is on the podium where stands the lectern. A pulpit or altar place is no more holy ground than where the seats for the people are placed.

I suppose it can be said that, in Religious Science and its teaching Science of Mind, the individual builds his own podium on which he can stand through Life, creating around him and from within him his own sanctuary. Here he is able to practice the peace that surpasseth all understanding, creating the love for others that he learns to have for himself. The platform and the auditorium are, as a whole, not built to separate the holy from the unholy.

It is the same with the bible, called the Holy Bible. In a court of law the witness places his hand on the Bible, supposedly to indicate that the book is a sacred text. Therefore, the vows of truth the person states become holy vows. In my family we were taught to never place another book on top of the Bible. The Bible was and is considered holy, that is, as sacred. Although thousands of bookstores sell bibles of all kinds to thousands of persons, we must realize that the message within the Bible is holy, even sacred, while the book itself is merely a printed book just as any printed book in any bookstore. The paper on which it is written is not holy—the message is. The Bible is a title of a book that contains many books and a bible is just a printed book that contains one or more stories. It could be said that all books could be bibles and some books are sacred to the individuals who have come to revere them. Enough of this.

There is a foundation for the structure of our church building that is not visible. That slab, that foundation, is as important to the actual building as are the front doors. Case in point: If the church building and interior decor are thought of as sacred, is not the concrete slab on which the building rests also holy? We revere structures and places. We designate "sacred sites," and then, in the next breath, we affirm that there is no place where God is not. This is incongruent.

Could not any place, then, be sacred?

I cite a statement by Dr. Albert Schweitzer, "Have reverence for all life." Once, I recall writing some notes for a Sunday lecture on the theme of revering all of Life. During my note-taking, a fly was really bugging me, and I kept brushing it away from my face. So engrossed was I in my notes that I automatically reached for a newspaper and began trying to swat the fly out of its existence. Suddenly, my eyes fell to my written note on the theme of my lecture. The whole thing quickly seemed rather silly—to be writing of the reverence for all Life and, in the same moment, attempting to swat the life out of one of God's creations. Needless to say, I allowed the fly to live out the rest of its time on the planet.

(But, of course, it may have chosen to irk someone else of lesser heart and heavier hand.)

All right then, the questions I pose are: What do you consider to be sacred? What is it you revere? What and who do you worship? What do you consider to be truly hallowed, holy? Take a few moments and think of what it is that is really sacred in your life experience.

Do you consider yourself sacred?

Yes, I mean you!

If you do not think yourself sacred, why not? It is written that Jesus said that the Kingdom of God is within you. To me that means that the God within you is not some shrine in a foreign land. That place within you is not a sacred site where people gather. It, God, is right there within you and within all the people who worship. It is written that Jesus also said, "He that sent me is with me."

What that means to me is that the Infinite Intelligence, the Divine Essence that created my body and my mind is still within me. It is that Divine Essence, that Divine Knowingness, that designed the hair on my left arm to lay to the left and the hair on my right arm to lay to the right. I certainly had nothing to do with it; my parents had nothing to do with it. They just accepted as their son that which had been designed for them by God.

(Ultimately, this particular design of God has ended up to be good for the parents, their son, and a great joy to the Designer.)

93

So, there is a sacredness that came with my beingness—a sacredness that is still within me, as it always shall be. "We may desecrate the body," someone said, "but we cannot truly destroy it."

Sacredness is that center of peace within each of us that is never in turmoil, never fettered, never in bondage, never sick or poor, never unhappy. That is that sacred "I" like the peace-filled eye of a hurricane that is always calm no matter how bad the storm circling around it is.

"Sacred" is to dedicate or to devote, we have learned. So, we must ask of ourselves, to what are we dedicating ourselves? To what are we devoting our time, our thoughts, our minds, and our lives? Let us hear from Emerson once again. "Tell me what you talk about all day long and I will tell you what you are and what you have," said the great American philosopher. And another American philosopher and minister, Tom Costa, adds, "Tell me what you are discussing or cussing and I will tell you what is happening in your life."

Buddha said, "What we dwell upon we become." Are we dwelling upon, or dedicating, or devoting our time and thoughts to misery? To pain? To sorrow? To joy? To happiness? Whichever or with all of the above, we are considering that which is to be sacred, for we are setting it apart and dwelling upon it.

Many people wish to get away from worshipping "things" in a particular religion or in a church. However, outside of the church, in their homes and lives, people begin worshipping other "things." Things such as money, liquor, cigarettes, and that long list of items that we revere and devote or to which we dedicate our very lives. So we have to ask ourselves what is at the top of our priority list? What is the dominant theme of devotion in our lives?

We must continually ask ourself, in meditation or in those quiet times we have with our self, "What is the dominant theme in our life?" If we come up with the feeling that we are worthy of Life, and if we consider ourself a sacred form and spirit, we can experience great good for ourselves.

I believe that people such as those reading this book, and other books on self-enlightenment and self-discovery, are in a re-dedication period in their lives. I believe you are re-setting your priorities, placing first those ideas and those inner changes that will improve and enhance that thing called "you" in that thing called Life.

Quite some time ago I counseled a young man to help him find the right therapy program for his alcoholism. He said to me, "Until I found this church and teaching, I did not know there was a different way to go or to live. I didn't realize that I actually had an alternative."

I relate easily to this young man discovering that there is an option and a choice of programs with ideas that can change a person's life. In my personal quest for self-respect, self-dignity, and self-love, that is truly the biggest step for me—knowing I have an alternative, another route of operation, another way to live.

The first part of my life I lived more or less like a Walter Cronkite TV news closing: "And that's the way it is." I accepted all of the dire things that were happening to me, not knowing they were perfect examples of the Law of Cause and Effect in action.

When I realized that there was an alternative, it was the "open sesame" idea that I needed in order to take charge of my life and to begin making changes. It didn't happen overnight. And it didn't happen in a very simple way. But in just knowing there was an option, doors began to open. And because I was looking for them, I slowly began to see that the key to these doors—all these doors of choice—was in my thinking. But as someone has said, "Have you ever noticed sometimes, when you struggle with your keys to unlock an unknown door, it is the last one on the ring that is the right one?"

Then I began to regard as sacred this ONEderful thing called Life; this glorious thing named "today." This really magnificent thing, this Universal Law called Cause and Effect is always in action, giving us the opportunity to change our lives.

I began to consider sacred the precious thing called Time. I have learned to respect the calendar, not to fear it. My happiest days have come in my so-called "twilight years." So now I anticipate the future, instead of fearing it. That was a great key when I began to consider sacred this moment of eternity called "now."

A few months ago, I was flying home to Palm Springs on a small airplane. We were in a rainstorm. It was the bumpiest trip I had ever experienced, and I had many fear-filled moments. On that plane a glorious lesson took place. When we landed safely I looked at my life as something very sacred. I saw my friend who came to meet the plane as someone sacred. When I arrived at home, my feeling toward my home was that it, too, was a sacred place. I will say many times that I know now you cannot be grateful and unhappy at the same time. It has become one of Costa's Laws.

The following morning, when I looked at my body, I considered it a magnificent creation of God. I thought of how careless I had been with this treasure, my body.

Gloria Swanson, who was a charter member of our church in Palm Desert, once said to me, "Tom, you are what you eat; you are what you think." She added, "This is not a garbage can," and pointed to her mouth.

I have learned that this treasurable thing, my body, really deserves to be taken care of. It is one of God's greatest gifts, and what we do with it is our gift to give back to God. If you do not take care of your Temple of God, who will? If you do not love your Temple of God, every organ, fiber, and cell, no one else will. I believe it was the comedian Jimmy Durante who said that famous line, "If I knew I were going to live this long, I would have taken much better care of myself."

I have learned, however, that it is best not to attempt to persuade other people into changing their eating or exercising habits. People rebel when you get on that subject. It is like getting your children to eat spinach because ". . .it is so good for you."

To the best of my human ability, I do not thrust my nutritional habits or ideas upon others. This is one of the easiest ways to lose friends, to alienate people, and to drive away church members. There is a well-known religion that almost went down the tubes because its founder was a vegetarian, insisting that ALL members of the sect also do the same. They left in droves until that directive was rescinded. Now, it is a very successful growing denomination.

The only right we have is to remind people that

their Temple of God, their vehicle of humanity, is sacred and ought to be treated as such. "We take much better care of our cars than we do our bodies," is an old but very true axiom. We would not dream of giving our dogs cigarettes or martinis. Our body is sacred! Let us choose to treat it and care for it as such, an instrument that needs love and care and continual tuning.

Our Mind is sacred. Our Life is sacred. Our Time is sacred. Is this not why a person who reveres himself, who loves himself, becomes a shining light for all to see? I do not mean kissing the mirror when you walk by. But realizing, when you look in your mirror, you see a force and power of great magnitude, greater than you, that created you!

Is it not true, too, that you respect someone who respects himself? We are attracted to people who have self-esteem. For me, those people are winners. When we care about ourselves, we are attracted to winners, and we have joy for those who are winning. I have never heard anyone in Las Vegas say, "Well, I am going to stay by this table and watch this person—he's a real loser!" You stand by and watch the person who is winning!

We are drawn to and are attracted to people who are confident and sure of themselves and what they are doing. All this boils down to the fact that, if you do not like yourself, you cannot expect anyone else to like you. If you do not trust yourself, how can you expect anyone else to trust you? What we think of ourselves is sacred! But if you try to analyze what other people think of themselves—*sacre bleu!*

A few years ago, I watched a television newscaster of a large eastern city interviewing muggers, their backs to the camera. Each of the thieves was asked what kind of people did they pick to mug? All four of the robbers agreed they would never go after someone who walked with certainty—with a confident pace. They would never mug a little old lady in sneakers, wearing long socks. It was likely that somewhere in her belongings there would be some sort of protective instrument. They stayed clear of people who appeared to know where they were and where they were going.

"Well, what type of person did you mug?" the newscaster asked.

They each replied, "The ones who walked with fear on their faces."

We have to believe in ourselves and what we are doing and what we are being in this life. If we do, the moral of the story becomes: We will not be chosen to be mugged.

Throughout all the ages every great teacher believed totally in their own beliefs—Jesus certainly did. Buddha certainly did. So, in reading spiritual, enlightening books that educate our mind and spirit about our selfhood, we have the opportunity to increase our belief in ourselves. Read books that lift you, inspire you, prod you, lead you to experience a daily search for self-respect and self-approval and self-love. Read books that tell you the methods of meditation, methods of organization, and of people who have developed themselves to be successful. And practice some of these teachings until they work for you or until you realize you need to search further for new methods of thought to implement new ideas in your life. And think on all of those attributes that succeed for others until they are absorbed completely.

When you are on the path of self-discovery, it really is difficult to turn back to an old way of thought, of just letting things happen as they will. Once you know how to turn on the light that is within, you cannot sit in the darkness of your mind. Oh, I suppose you could try, but eventually the new knowledge of self-appreciation will seep through. And there, in the mind, is that light shining—and it is a light seen by all those with whom you come in contact. Dr. Holmes once said that the most frustrated people in the world have to be metaphysicians because they know what they must do, but they won't do it. I've been there, and I know the feeling.

Many of us are not ready for the truth. We once had a sign in the foyer of our church that read: "Truth spoken here; bring your own containers." How true that is. Each person gleans what they choose to experience, to negate, to accept, to believe, or to deny.

Again, I repeat. What do we hold sacred? What do we revere? Are we devoted to our story? Our illness? Our pain? Our misery? Our lack? Are we dedicating ourselves to that hurt, the unkind remark? That divorce? The job you "got fired from?"

What is the dominant theme in your life? What is the *leitmotif*—the strain that is the thread of the symphony of your life? What is the tune of Life that we keep playing? To turn a phrase from *My Fair Lady*, "The pain and strain is mainly in the brain." What are we holding so dear in our lives? Why are we continuing to remember the raw deal we got fifteen years ago? Maybe it was raw because we did not allow it to ripen! Whatever it is, you have set it apart and devoted yourself to it. Now it becomes a sacred place of sacrifice—sacrificing that precious thing called Time.

Let us examine what we spend our time dwelling upon. Let us realize, you and I, that we are sacred. The home you live in is sacred; the place you work in and the work you perform is sacred. I know there are some who will quake at that last statement, but let me remind those who are still cringing at the things I say, "Churning is learning."

Along with this concept of what is sacred, I cite the example of the famous statue by Michelangelo, the *Pieta*, resting in the Vatican. It is a famous marble statue depicting Mary holding in her arms the body of Jesus after the crucifixion.

In actuality, the marble has become worn because over a period of years countless millions have touched it constantly, reverently. Worshipers believe it to be a sacred object—their touch tender, an expression of deep emotion. But, is it not strange to say that when a stranger reaches out to touch the hand of so many, it is likely they will cringe, withdraw?

How very strange are we humans. We can touch and revere a piece of cold marble depicting human forms, but we cannot revere another human expression of God, a precious object created by the Great Intelligence. Is it reverent to touch an inanimate object in order to receive some healing benefit, but irreverent to hold the hand of a stranger and sing, "Let there be peace on earth...?"

How many persons have kissed the Blarney stone and yet refrained from kissing an actual person— even on the cheek? In my book, that is a lot of "blarney." What does the First Commandment say? "There shall be no false gods before me." Are not statues "false gods?"

I had a friend who is on the Alcoholics Anonymous program. He said, "I gave up a false god, the bottle. He played tricks on me. Now I have the real God I can depend upon." What a marvelous example this is of how we consider things outside ourselves sacred in the avoidance of looking within ourselves for that which is truly sacred—that which is holy.

"Now we are sons of God!" Jesus said.

My beloved ones, you ARE sacred to the Divine Plan of the Universe. Give yourself permission to accept your sacredness.

8

Heavy, Heavy What Hangs Over You?

Remember the child's game called "Heavy, Heavy, What Hangs Over You?" We played it often back in Pennsylvania where I was raised. It was a cute game. Someone would hold an object over a playmate's head and ask the question, "Heavy, heavy, what hangs over you?" A playmate would offer some guesses of the object being held over his head—a stone, a rock, a pencil, a toy, a piece of clothing.

Personally, I believe I continued to play that game throughout my teens (my awful teens), my adulthood, both early and middle (at the present moment I refuse to define later adulthood). My game-playing was an attempt to guess what burdens weighed me down. What heavy clouds of gloom and doom hung over me preventing me from seeing the sun and feeling light in my heart.

My mind flashes to that glorious graphic example of a father and son walking along the beach. The little boy keeps picking up little pebbles of various sizes, shapes, and colors, stuffing them into the pockets of his jeans. After a time, he has collected so much that his overloaded pockets make it difficult for him to walk. The boy asks his father to carry him.

The father picks up the boy. By this time, with many rocks, pebbles, and stones in his jeans, the boy is too heavy for the father's arms. "Son, I am willing to carry you," the father says, "but first you must take all the stones and rocks out of your pockets." He sets the boy down.

Symbolically, this father represents the Heavenly Father, the Creative Intelligence of the Universe. You and I are that child. We have all walked along the beach of Life; we have picked up a few heavy stones, have we not? We have picked up rocks of doubt, the stones of fear, some pebbles of resentment. We have placed them in the pockets of our consciousness—that mental receptacle that is our subconscious mind, the seat of our memory.

Those things—rocks, stones, pebbles—are what weigh us down. Then, in our pain, our weariness, our despair, we turn to the Father within and we cry out, "Help me!" We shout for help to make it through the night or the day. The Father within us says, "Put down the rocks, my child. I would like to carry you through this, but there are too many stones, too many rocks of disbelief—too many rocks of doubt. I will carry you when you lay down that doubt, fear, and the resentment. Put all of them aside, and when your burden is light I shall carry you."

Is this why, when we pray so often to be free of the load, we do not receive an answer? Can the stones be reasons why our thinking is not clear? Jesus, it is written, spoke of these very matters. "Remove the beam from your own eye before you attempt to remove it from the eye of your brother," he said.

Prayer, Spiritual Mind Treatment, is our mind tool to remove the obstacles, the ". . . beam in the eyes of others." Spiritual Treatment—that is, prayer scientifically spoken—is our tool to cleanse us of the rocks that thwart our good. An interesting way of looking at the child and father on the beach is seeing it symbolically—to let go of the problem is to see the answer.

Many times when I do a crossword puzzle I become stymied over a definition. I cannot see the finish so I lay down the puzzle and proceed to do something else for awhile. When I return to the puzzle, I view it from another angle, a fresh perspective. I think to myself, why could I not see that earlier? I had to move away from the proverbial forest to see the differences in the trees. This is true with our lives.

Therefore, in whatever puzzle you are facing, perhaps the pieces that are not fitting in are the ones that do not fit despite our insisting that they will. In the jigsaw puzzle of Life, we cannot shave the edges of the various pieces to make them fit. Every piece of the puzzle has its rightful place in the whole picture. So applying this idea to our mosaic of Life, perhaps we are insisting on certain people staying in our viewpoint of Life's patterns. You know within that they do not need to stay.

If we apply this to our theme, Heavy, Heavy. . ., some of the pieces of puzzle are not needed. Yet, the pieces, as stones and rocks, become nonetheless too heavy a load for us to bear. We must let go of the rocks that have been rocking our boat! We must disallow the very thought of the rocks and pebbles that have kept us "stoned" physically and emotionally. Forgiveness is letting go. Perhaps we need to forgive a stone or two that has been a heavy burden. Ask yourself what rocks you carry around that make Life so heavy. Are there any rocks of unforgiveness? Those rocks can get you down on your knees. Are you carrying a rock of fear, of doubt, of anxiety? If you are, you will be immobilized by these thoughts. It will not be easy for you to move out of the situation that you say you want to move out of.

Our load is made easy when we rid our pockets of consciousness of heavy memories, those heavy judgments, those heavy stones of grudge and resentment. If there is one excuse why you will not let go of your problem, of "What he did to you," of "What she said" about you, then the Father within cannot carry you through that dark, heavy valley. Your rocks might justify you, but they will not heal you.

However small, only you know which pebbles you have to release, to let go of, and to throw out into the Universe. When you diminish your rock pile, watch your life improve.

A worthy, interesting question to ask ourselves is "Do we want to be justified, or do we wish to be healed?" Take your pick. It is impossible to be both justified and healed. Only that unseen part of you, your memory, carries around all those heavy things, that pain, that hurt, that "look-what-they-did-to-me" feeling.

Forgive. Disallow. Let go!

In addition, we must cease the practice—that's what it is, a practice—of carrying around other people's rocks and loads. I have counseled many people (including myself) who have, or are suffering from, guilt because they faced the problem of being forced to place their mother or father in a convalescent home because their parents' condition required constant care. When I faced this decision, the membership in my church was around four hundred people. So I had to be realistic and choose one of the options: Either I devote my life to taking care of my mother, whose stroke totally incapacitated her, or I devote myself and ministry to leading and caring for those four hundred people. With those odds, my sister and I chose to place our mother in a clean convalescent facility near my home.

However, heavy, HEAVY was the guilt that followed the action. Although I dashed over to see her nearly every day, it was sad but true that she did not know whether I had been with her or not. This was a large rock on my heart for more than two years. I watched a dear, kind person turn into a disheveled human being before my eyes.

That rock had to be released without any guilt. That place and the care she received were the best for her at that time. My sister and I took the responsibility for what others would think, judge, or say about our decision.

We must stop carrying around the rocks of our friends, or our children, or our spouses. This doesn't mean we break the connection with them or be unconcerned about them, but to know the difference between worry, anxiety, and concern. As in the Serenity Prayer, now so familiar: ". . .accept the things I cannot change, and change the things I can."

Dr. Raymond Charles Barker once said (he no doubt said it many times) that more family problems have been solved by keeping your hands out of the individual problems of the family. I quite agree. There are some rocks that we cling to for strength, for purpose, for enhancement, but the only rock that has benefited any of us is the eternal rock of all the ages—the Universal Power called God.

Years ago a tailor gave me a simple lesson that applies to many life attributes. "Tom, if you want to take care of your clothing, your good suits, and you want them to look good and last longer, at night, before you hang up the suit you have been wearing, take everything out of the pockets. That will help keep its shape."

Our lives and our minds are like good suits. When we go to bed at night, we need to take everything out of the pockets of our consciousness. This will help our life keep its shape. I have said repeatedly, "Why lose sleep at midnight about money when the banks do not open until ten o'clock the next day?" What did Scarlett say to Rhett Butler? "Frankly, Rhett, I will not think about that now. I will think about that tomorrow!"

(And we might add a couple of fiddle-de-dees to that one.)

Yesterday, with its worries, ought to be gone! Make last night a completed experience. It is over, gone, done with, *kaput!*

Each New Year's Eve we count down the minutes and the last seconds of the "old" year. When the clock strikes the first note of midnight we toot horns and revel over the old year's passing away while welcoming the new one upon us. There are those who may have greater wisdom. They retire at ten o'clock, saying "Goodbye old year." They awaken the next morning saying, "Hello new year." This is the kind of thing we can do each night when we retire. We can toot horns and revel over this one day ending, shouting praises for a new day's beginning. Our sleep is our great restorer. Our prayer, each thought we have, is that great restorer. If we can agree that every minute is the great opportunity for our restoration, then whatever the day is, as hectic and as challenging as it may be, as glorious as it may be, it is over with when we close our eyes for sleep.

One of Costa's Laws is that, if there is anything heavy hanging over you, the night is the time to let go of it. As you try to fall asleep, think of your world as a white light—the trying will end, the sleep will come.

At night take everything out of your consciousness just like you take things out of the pockets of your suit. Remove anything that obstructs you that day, anything that slows you down, impedes your happiness, anything that weighs you down. Forgiveness is the best method to achieving Divine restoration. This is very much like hanging up your clothes. The wrinkles go away; the shape is restored.

When people come to me to discuss something of importance to them they enter with "rocks in their heads." Now, where else could those stones and rocks be except in their thinking, their consciousness, their hearts? So we in the counseling field help them to help themselves relieve their burdens, their spiritual and mental rocks.

So often I see people who enter my office actually stooped over with the weight of their world upon their shoulders. And with absolutely nothing other than being given a new thought, a new idea, they walk away as if they had just spent time at a health farm.

(And, of course, they have!)

What causes them to straighten up and walk tall? Only thought—for that is the only heavy, heavy thing that has been hovering over them.

It is written the teacher Jesus said, "If I but be lifted up, I draw all men unto me." This is the theme, the axiom, the basis of every consultation a minister has: To lift the people up who enter with their heavy pain of memories, resentments, and grudges; to help them drop the rocks.

We have heard the story of Jesus walking on water. For me, walking on water is, symbolically, walking above appearances. Water represents Spirit. Therefore, Spirit as subjective mind is cause for us to rise above the appearances and judge not by them. We are, then, consciously walking upon the water. We then dedicate these ideas to those men and women who still carry rocks. We urge them to give up their rock collections. Drop those stones as did the little boy who wished to be carried in the arms of his father. Those stones are merely burdened, heavy thoughts.

Many times a divorce becomes a heavy rock. A person says he cannot forgive the spouse whom he married. For years, a painful memory becomes a rock that weighs him down. Forgiveness is a way of removing this feeling of jealousy. Jealousy, like acid, will eat its own container.

The death experience of a loved one, or as we call it, "a transition," can be a large rock. Certainly grief is a strong stone to carry. It becomes that heavy cloud of loss that hangs over us and affects all the areas of our lives. We cannot resume our life, for that cloud of grief takes over, ever hovering over us. It takes its toll physically, emotionally, and mentally.

Dr. Ernest Holmes says, "Fear is nothing more than misplaced faith." He adds that there are three fears that can be devastating to our growth and prevent us from living a happy life. One is the fear of lack, when we believe that God, the Infinite Intelligence, will not supply us with all that we need. Second, the fear of death, for we are not convinced of our own mortality or the mortality of others. And third, the fear of loss, the loss of health, friends, property.

Loss can be a heavy rock. Loss of a beloved one, loss of a job, loss of money. It is said that many times, when there is a loss of a loved one, the surviving spouse will grieve himself or herself to their own grave or into extreme illness.

So, look at your fears. Someone said one time, an acronym for the word "fear" is False Evidence Appearing Real. Fear can be a heavy, heavy that hangs over us for years or for a lifetime. "Do that which you fear and you remove the fear," Emerson said over a century ago. How light can be our lives when we become objective about our fears and see them for what they really are—temporary heavy thoughts.

A woman had horrible nightmares, the same event happening over and over in her dreams. She would dream that an enormous green dragon was chasing her, and she would become frantic. Then, just about the time the dragon was catching up to her, she would awaken in a cold sweat.

One night, she did not awaken in time and the dragon caught her. There she was in the clutches of this dragon, steam jetting from its nostrils (just like in a horror movie). The woman was in sheer panic. So she looked up at the dragon and screamed, "What are you going to do with me?"

The dragon replied, "I don't know, lady. It's your dream!"

Funny? I think so.

However, when we apply this tale to our own lives, we realize that we create our own monsters, and only we can decide what damage the ogres are going to do. We are able to conjure up the heavy or the light, the feared or the fearless, the panic or the peace. There is a science of chaos, and we see it all about us. There is, too, a science and an art to a peaceful experience. Whatever dragon or monster we have dragged into our life, we can "UNdrag" it; we can create something else out of the same substance called Mind—our wonderful mind.

This is the time to look at the "heavies" in our lives. Is it not interesting to observe how various persons handle their several rocks and stones?

One of my prize students has had cerebral palsy since she was a youngster. However, her attitude toward her dis-ease is sensational. She considers it an inconvenience, but in no way does she think of herself as handicapped. She is able to drive a car. She works in a local hospital assisting other people with their "inconveniences." She manages her life totally on her own.

One day in a class she shared the classic example of her independence—how she handles her "rocks." She was taking ballet lessons. Some of her classmates gasped a bit at this news, some strained to hold back a giggle. Most could not believe what they heard.

She told us that, on a particular day of one of her ballet classes, she couldn't manage a turn. However, two days later she was able to do the dance turn easily.

Her ballet instructor asked her why it was that two days earlier she could not do it, and suddenly she was able to manage it extremely well.

"I forgot I couldn't do it," she replied.

Now, let us imagine the moments we could forget we could not do something. Imagine how it could be if we could forget about those heavy rocks once and for all. Those of us in that classroom learned a great deal from the brave lady about Life and inconveniences, handling rocks, our heavy thoughts.

"Heavy, Heavy..." is an important concept to me. On the day I lectured this topic—"Heavy, heavy, what hangs over you?"—a life changed. One woman attending church, hearing this idea, could not admit she had a problem with alcohol. Her husband had brought her to church that day. Something magical in this idea, some spiritual hook, latched onto her thought process. That same evening she attended her first Alcoholics Anonymous meeting. She has not taken a drink in several years now. So, I am grateful for having presented these ideas in lecture. I am gratified these ideas redeemed a life—that it helped to change the thought and direction of just one person. However, I do know others are helped by good ideas to pass through that valley, to step over the rockpile of obstructions.

I open all my classes with a phrase I learned: "I am a valuable, worthwhile person." Knowing that lives may change from what you say or what you may write is one of the fringe benefits of being in this teaching ministry. It is worthy to help people to know that they are worthy human beings—that they count in God's plan. Life can be light. We need only believe this to make it a truth.

ONE DAY AT A TIME
by
Ralph Waldo Emerson

Finish every day and be done with it. You have done what you could. Some blunders and absurdities no doubt crept in; forget them as soon as you can. Tomorrow is a new day; begin it well and serenely and with too high a spirit to be cumbered with your old nonsense. This day is all that is good and fair. It is too dear, with its hopes and invitations, to waste a moment on the yesterdays.

9

Bless or Be Less

When someone sneezes have you considered why we say, "God bless you?" I asked this question one Sunday morning during my lecture. In the reception line, at the end of the service, I received several varied explanations and meanings.

One version was: When you sneeze, all the body functions momentarily cease, and at that time, it is the closest thing to death that we may experience. "God bless you" is, more or less, a "welcome back!"

Another person told me that the Devil was being released in the sneezing process, and the blessing prodded the Devil to quickly leave the body—keeping him at bay, I suspect.

Another explanation was: When you sneeze you are getting rid of someone. I have sneezed hundreds of times in the last few decades—I am amazed I still have many people in my life.

Noted author and Religious Science minister/practitioner, Dr. Raymond Charles Barker has said that a sneeze is letting go of a bad idea.

So many varied, colorful tales—somewhat like receiving prescriptions from a pharmacy. I listened to these explanations and thanked each person for sharing what they believed to be true for them. But which tale is correct—which is "true?" I certainly don't know.

(I don't believe any of these versions would apply as answers in a trivia game.)

Let us examine this idea of blessing and what it means.

According to some theologians, the idea of blessing with holy water came from an old Egyptian agricultural ritual that is pagan in origin. Research into this tells us that, in the ancient days of Egypt, there was a ritual ceremony for fertility that happened the same time each year, at the beginning of the spring season.

As the winter became spring and the fields were being prepared for sowing crops, there was a specially chosen group who boarded a flat barge to sail down the river—Mother Nile. Ceremoniously a leader or high priest dipped a long wand into the river, then flicked the water from both sides of the barge, sprinkling the land on either side.

The sole purpose of the ritual was to ensure the fertility of the fields. It had absolutely nothing to do with religion, although later it somehow crept into religious, ceremonial rites.

Delving into the meaning of the word "blessing," we can see some subjective connection with the purpose of the ritual. "Blessing," most dictionaries tell us, means "to guard, to protect, to encourage, to approve, to praise, to glorify." In the glossary of the textbook, *Science of Mind*, by Dr. Ernest Holmes, founder of the Religious Science movement, "Blessing is any constructive thought that is directed toward anyone, or any condition."

Saying it another way, you bless someone when you recognize the divinity within a person, a place, or a thing. For instance, if I think well of your business, I am blessing you. If I am thinking rightly of you, then I am blessing you. If I am thinking rightly of a condition or some happening, perhaps thinking rightly of a problem, I am blessing it.

(Here "rightly" means, affirmatively, in a positive fashion, realistically and creatively, as with a learning opportunity.)

You may extend this idea to the act of encouraging someone. When you pat someone on the back or when you are approving toward some person, then you are blessing them. When you are assisting someone in realizing who and what they are, you are blessing them. Blessing, then, is to awaken something in the atmosphere of thought. "Stir up the embers of God within you!" the Bible tells us.

So, as we awaken the divine possibilities in us, confirming our divine potential, we are giving ourselves a blessing. We are thinking rightly, stirring up the God within.

"Man is God asleep. God is man awake," Dr. Erwin Seale has said. In looking at this idea squarely, I must think rightly of you. If I am not encouraging you, not approving of you, then I am not blessing you. Therefore, in withholding encouragement and approval, I shall be less than the truth that I am.

I shall be less than God intended me to be if I am not seeing the divinity within you and within myself. So comes the question: "Shall I bless or be less?"

A few months ago when I was on the East Coast, I worked on this idea for a segment of a seminar I conducted. Early on the morning of the first day, I explored many of these thoughts and placed them on paper. In the midst of this process, I realized I needed to eat something before the seminar. I took up my notes and went downstairs to the hotel's restaurant for breakfast. I had been in the restaurant business for many years and had a great deal of experience waiting on tables. It is really habit that causes me to observe waiters and waitresses—especially with regard to considerations for the tip.

While waiting to give my breakfast order—also the pouring of my first cup of coffee and the filling of the water glass—I found myself observing a waitress who was, obviously, new in her profession. I became all involved in judgment. I marveled at her inefficiency. "Why doesn't she get that man's order?" I said to myself. "Why doesn't she bring the toast to that lady at the next table?" I thought. "She's almost finished her omelette."

I became so involved in something that I judged I needed to be involved in—except to have *my* order taken. Suddenly, I looked at my seminar notes on the table (or should I say, the notes looked up at me!). I realized that I was experiencing exactly what I had been writing and the ideas I was to speak about at the seminar an hour later. I was certainly being less than I could be.

Shall I bless or be less?

At that moment I certainly felt less than God intended me to be, as long as I sat in judgment. I was not looking for the divinity within this waitress.

Mentally, I began to practice what I would be "preaching" an hour later. I began blessing this waitress. Suddenly, I observed her as a human being attempting to perform at her best. I saw she was doing as well as she knew how at that moment. Instead of seeing a fumbling girl, one I surely would never hire in my restaurant, I saw a professional at her best!

What I learned from this experience was another lesson in patience. I learned that, when we are into judgment, we become less. Is there a person reading this who has not felt this "less-ness" in their daily lives? Unhappiness is always a part of "less-ness."

Shortly after I changed my feeling and began to bless this waitress, she came to my table and took my order. When she served my meal a few minutes later, I smiled at her. She returned a warm smile to me.

This was quite a change for me. I had sat there with my earlier judgment, and I had determined I was *not* going to tip her one thin dime. As it came about later, I over-tipped—and I enjoyed it! This was my subtle way of blessing her and of thinking rightly about this lovely waitress. Later, when I told the story of the frazzled waitress who suddenly became a person with my blessing bestowed upon her, many people told me they identified with my feeling.

I learned that *blessing* can *be* a blessing.

As I continued to develop these ideas, I created my own personal rosary of gratefulness. I have discovered that you cannot be grateful and unhappy at the same time. It is just impossible. List your many gratitudes one by one—these are blessings undisguised. As we begin to count our individual blessings (not someone else's blessings on us), it is amazing how many blessings we find to count.

Does this mean that we must bless where we are? Does this mean we have to bless our problem? Do we bless the adverse conditions we are moving through? Does it mean we have to bless that terrible job we are in? Do we bless all the people in our lives—good or bad?

The answer is a resounding "Yes!"

To explain this, I refer once again to Emmett Fox and his distinction between the right place and true place. He said that many times the student of metaphysics will say to the practitioner or to the minister: "Pray for my right place."

We recall Dr. Fox maintains that your right place could be the hospital that you just entered. You are there to receive your physical healing. The hospital is your right place for now. However, it certainly is not your true place. To a prisoner, the jail could be the right place for right now, but it is certainly not his true place.

Let us apply that idea to us.

Our problem, our "shadowed valley," could be our right place until we learn our lesson and work our way through it. But this doesn't mean it is our true place. Our true place is out of the valley, the shadow we call the "problem." Our right place is right where we are, in order to solve the problem, in order to grow emotionally and spiritually.

"We can learn through intuition and through suffering," Dr. Holmes said, "but most people feel they have to learn through suffering, and therefore they do." Allowing suffering to be your right place as a time to learn leads you to your true place. So let us return to the idea of blessing.

If we bless our problem, heavy and insurmountable as it may seem—if we think rightly of it—then we can clearly think our way out of it. The chaos and confusion that go with condemnation, judgment, fear, and doubt do not allow one to think with clarity.

Many lives can be improved by a blessing of your "exes." I have said many times, "You bless yourself when you bless your ex-husband, ex-wife, ex-boss, your ex-friend." Blessing is a form of forgiveness; it takes you out of the past, out of the pain, out of the memory and back into the present. Blessing will move you onward with your life. Without the blessing, without the forgiveness, one may become stuck in the muck and mire of the "things" that got you there in the first place.

Jealousy is a result of being stuck in your own opinion or judgment. Jealousy always makes you inferior to that toward which you are jealous.

Greed is counting someone else's rosary of blessings.

Envy is the mud that you sling at your own potential.

Joy, peace, and love, is the result of finding your own truth.

So the question we have to ask ourselves is, "Shall we bless or shall we be less?" That is, to be less than the magnificent creation of God that we already are?

In my daily life, I bless my bills. I suggest everyone do so. After all, we are the ones who created them. Why not bless the electric company or the gas company? Those companies keep you cool in the summer and warm in the winter. Let's face it, who turned the rheostat on, up, and down?

Why become upset and throw your hands into the air in despair when you receive a bill for something you bought four weeks ago? Bless your bills. That means, of course, think rightly of them.

Before you deposit your money in the bank and any time you handle it, bless it. You might find yourself reading what is printed on American dollar denominations, "In God We Trust." Your money serves you, blessing all your choices and decisions. Dr. Raymond Charles Barker has written, "Money is God in action." And Dr. Tom Costa adds his own blessing "Amen, Dr. Barker."

That funny thing called "money." Who is there among us seeing an old beat up, filthy, crumpled one-hundred-dollar bill (or even a ten-dollar bill) on the ground, who would not pick it up and put it in our pocket? Not I, for one. I think of once hearing someone say that money has no home. It just comes in to visit for awhile and then goes on its way to serve again. Have you noticed that money always goes where it is respected and where it is treated well. Handle your money positively, creatively, and wisely. And bless it!

For many years, I have always written on every check that I write—even if I am in a hurry—FIDGET FATIM. This is something I took up when learning about a metaphysical affirmation that someone else coined for themselves. I could never remember it because there were too many consonants in the affirmation. It was like reading an eye chart. So I juggled it around and came up with "fidget fatim." It means, "Father, I do give eternal thanks for abundance that is mine."

Countless people who have heard this have taken to this act of prosperity, writing "fidget fatim" on their checks. This, to me, is an exercise of subjectifying, blessing the person or the organization I am paying—including the church I support. This is thinking well of them. This is thinking rightly of the service for which I contract, the merchandise that I purchase, and the items that I choose to bring into my home.

This is a blessing for the food I have in my kitchen. When I write "fidget fatim" on the check that buys the food items in the supermarket, it is as if I am blessing the farmer who grows the fruits or vegetables. It is my blessing to the market for bringing it to me; it is saying grace before the food is eaten, before it is placed on the table, before it even gets to the market. It is my way of blessing what I have chosen to take home with me.

At times, in seminars and in classes I teach, I begin the course by passing among the students a bill of any denomination. I tell the group that I would like them to accept this money in their hands, to look at it for a brief moment, to think well of it, to bless it, and then release it. Let it go. "When someone taps you on the shoulder and hands you the bill, it is totally unexpected," I tell the class. "So bless it, think rightly of it. It is yours. It is in your life for a short moment. Then, at the perfect time, you allow it to move out of your life."

The thing that is happening is that you energize the feeling of circulation, the very key and the basis for the world's economy, while doing the same with your own personal world. It is the basis for our body, the Temple of God that we use on this planet. It is God circulating among us, offering us the Universal Abundance.

Then I remind the people doing this exercise that, whether it is money, a car, a job, a house, a friend, or a loved one, accept all of them into your life, bless them for the brief time they are there, and when the time to release comes, let them go.

Nothing comes into your life to stay forever in physical form. You do not stay in the lives of others in physical form, nor do I. We move through Life, through the lives of others, as people also move through our lives. There is truth in the quote, "And it came to pass that Divine Mind created our Spiritual Self out of Itself in order to come to pass through the experience of growth so that we may, with our new knowledge and the lessons learned, pass on to another experience, to again come to pass."

So bless all there is in your life and experience while it is there. I flash to the multiplication story in the Bible. The story goes that Jesus, faced with the challenge of feeding the multitudes who had gathered to hear him, had only a few fish and loaves of bread. He blessed these things and looked up at the crowds of five thousand people. You know what happened—the fishes and the loaves multiplied. The food baskets seemed continually full as they were passed to the people. In the end there were still left twelve baskets full of food. More than enough surplus. This was abundance, my friends. It was not "just enough."

Writing the Lamsa Bible, a translation from the Aramaic, Dr. George Lamsa has an interesting version of this story. Dr. Lamsa, who spoke Aramaic, which was the native tongue of Jesus, intimates that, in the original translation of the story, what really happened was that a great many merchants in the area, approving of the good work that Jesus was doing, realized he was to speak to a large group of people who were bound to be hungry.

So the merchants gathered up their camels and sent provisions to the place where Jesus was to speak. When the leaders had asked Jesus what they could do to feed this large gathering with so very little food at hand, Jesus "created" the food— blessing the meager foods before him, praying for supply. The camels arrived at this moment, and the "miracle" that he could provide food for five thousand people was just a Divine out-working, an out-picturing, of the Law that Jesus invoked in his prayer for abundance and supply.

Of course, most people would rather have the dramatic, even sensational, version of the event that would once again set Jesus apart as the great exception instead of the great example of Divine Mind.

I am inclined to agree with Dr. Lamsa, that the prayer given by Jesus was the Divine Law working divinely.

Bless what you are; bless what you have, or you shall be less than you are. Bless the clothes you wear, the car you drive, the place where you live, all your accounts, payables and receivables— acknowledge and bless all the people once in your life, acknowledge and bless all the people now in your life, and those who may yet come into your life. All are right for your life at the time they are in your experience.

Bless or be less!

Be no less than magnificent, no less than perfect, no less than divine.

My blessing is upon you.

And I gratefully accept your blessing.

10

Batteries
Not Included

When driving, I like to speak ideas into my tape recorder. Then, when I arrive home, I listen to the tape and write down material that I might use in my talks. The gist of my comments are sometimes sketchy, probably dependent on how much concentration I have spent on driving. Then again, at other times, I seem to flower a full-blown lecture, which can mean I was spending a good deal of driving time sitting at stop signs or traffic lights. The reason I do this is because, when you are away from the forest, you can see clearly the large aspects of landscape.

(I'm certain you would want me to avoid using a cliche—you thought I would say, "I can see the trees.")

It is the same with leadership of a church—in fact, I am confident that brief absences from any business may assist in perceiving the truth of things. It does a person good to get away, so that he can look at his enterprise with different eyes. Such long-range view assists in gaining new perspectives.

When I am not *on* the church grounds at Palm Desert, I can often observe what needs to be done *with* the church grounds.

One day, while driving and recording my ideas, the recorder stopped. It just stopped! So I dropped into a local store and bought a new one, leaving the old one to be repaired. While I was in the store, I looked over several different kinds and makes of recorders—and a few other technical items that caught my fancy. I noticed that many of the recording devices had a little tag with a notation that said, "batteries not included."

A few days later, while reading the newspaper, my eyes fell upon a local store's doll sale. Again, I noted a little asterisk, which directed my eye to the bottom of the advertisement—it said, "batteries not included." And a very few days after that I saw an advertisement in the movie section of the paper that promoted a film entitled, "Batteries Not Included."

Since I am always on the lookout for a title and theme for my Sunday lectures and lessons, I realized that I was being prodded, actually stimulated by this idea: BATTERIES NOT INCLUDED.

The title stayed with me, although I had no concept what the metaphysical connection might be. I knew I was getting a message to get a message.

The more I mused on the thought, the more I became amused with what was coming out of the blue for my upcoming talk. I placed the title firmly on the list of forthcoming lectures and went on to think about it in the broadest terms.

My first reaction was how could this idea, "batteries not included," have anything to do with a Sunday morning talk? After a short while I realized there was a strong link connecting an instrument needing batteries with the power source linking us to the One Source. I realized also that no matter how intricately some instruments were designed, how marvelous their function, they needed energy to perform; they needed batteries to operate effectively. These rather magnificent recording instruments are shells, quite empty and meaningless—unless, of course, a battery is inserted into them.

We, you and I, are sometimes like these instruments. We are magnificently and divinely created. Our bodies are technical, intricate mechanisms of Life. Yet, sometimes we are just shells, empty of

134

purpose, of direction, and of intent.

Oh, we may pretty-up the shells. We may have face-lifts, nose jobs, new hair-dos, new glasses, contact lenses—we may preoccupy ourselves with activities at the local gym. We may adorn the shell with Christian Dior dresses, Yves Saint Laurent suits, Rolex watches, and all the usual expensive "frou-frou," as I call it. We add baubles, bangles, and beads to this shell, but inside, there is no meaningful energy—there may be no life at all.

On some occasions we are like the jack o'lantern, the empty pumpkin the day after Halloween—the light has been blown out and it sits there with a silly grin with no light from within. On All Saints' Day, November first, it's all gone!

At one time, my own life was once like that. I perceive now that I was just a shell. I possessed all the outside accoutrements: the cars, the trips, the bank account, the houses, the etceteras, but not much else. Then one day I awakened, more or less, to find myself hearing the words of the famous Peggy Lee song: "Is That All There Is?" My life, I thought, was without meaning—quite lifeless in fact.

By way of example I like to tell the story about a time when I was driving down the main street of Palm Desert. I noticed a young lady standing on the edge of the road beside a gorgeous white Silver Cloud Rolls Royce. At first glance I thought she was one of the members of our church.

I pulled over to the side of the road to see if she needed assistance. However, when I approached her, I recognized she was not a church member. In any event, being caught in the helping-the-helpless frame of mind, I said, "May I help you?"

"I'm out of gas," the young woman replied sheepishly. "I'm sorry," she added in apology.

Out of gas? I thought, a Rolls Royce, OUT OF GAS!

Suddenly, the incongruity of it all struck me, metaphysically. For here at the side of the road, motionless, was this magnificent hand-crafted piece of machinery, hand-tooled, every detail perfectly designed and executed by the great car craftsmen of England. The leather seats were like silk, the chrome shining in the desert sun more than chrome shining anywhere in the world—that is, a grand vehicular creation costing ninety thousand dollars—out of gas!!!

> *(My first thought was to inquire of the young lady just what was her annual car insurance premium. I thought later on that, of all the countless times I have been in service stations for gas to refuel my own car, I have never once seen a Rolls Royce in a gas station being refueled! Have you? Where do Rolls Royce owner's get gas?)*

Anyway, I went back to my car and drove to the nearest gas station. I purchased a gallon of gas and returned to the Rolls. I put the gas in the tank, and the lady said, "Oh, thank you so much," and off she went into the desert sunshine.

> *(I do hope she went back to the gas station to fill up her gas tank—I have no idea what mileage a Rolls Royce gets.)*

Now, coming back to our idea, let us apply this scene to us, to our bodies, our minds, our lives.

God, the one Divine Creator, has perfectly designed our bodies. I have never seen anyone with a nose on their elbow or an eye on their hip. God, the Great Designer, knew exactly where to put everything in order to provide the right balance—to make everything perfect and useful.

In daily life, we adorn this special creation with gold lamé—garments made from imported fabrics. Yet often, too often, something is missing. There is no spark, despite the gold that glitters. There is no animation despite the wonderful, colorful fabrics. We may exist this way, but are we living when we do? If not, why not?

Are batteries included in this package? Is there something that can motivate a lifeless form, such as this body of ours, into creative action?

Of course, the answer is "Yes." Yes, a thousand times yes!

It is Mind—our consciousness.

Our mind is the battery that sparks us and prods us to go in a certain direction. It is also the same mind that can drive us to, and up, the walls! Our mind is greater than our outer shell. Our mind, that special thing that is what we truly are, that separates each of us as a unique individual, is much more than our job, our house, or our money in the bank. We are much more than a bag of bones covered over with a garment called "flesh." We are God-Mind individualized, and while One with all there is, our individuality is the reflection of our collective Mind.

For so many years I lived like a little Barbie doll—a Tommy doll—crying out, "Mommy and Daddy." I strove for what I called "independence," but it seemed I came from a state of defiance and rebellion—not from a state of consciousness that was clear and free. Defiance is a conditioned state of contempt for what we perceive as opposite.

When I left home at age sixteen, I thought I cut the umbilical cord. Really, all I was doing was stretching it cross-country to California. And then, after I arrived here with my statements of freedom from my home, I spent my time looking for someone to plug the stretched umbilical into.

I established what I thought was independence, little realizing I was setting up my standards according to the opposite of what my father stood for. As an example, my father took his coffee with cream and sugar. I made sure I drank black coffee. My father loved bananas. I didn't eat one until I was thirty-five years old. I would become ill at the smell of a banana split. Whatever my father had done, whatever he liked or disliked, I would be certain to do the opposite.

Then one day I found out that this was defiance, not independence. For the record, I enjoy bananas now. I drink coffee as often with cream and sugar as I drink it black.

Still, for years I did not make a move unless someone pushed me into action. When I found my spiritual battery, my own consciousness, which had always been with me, I became activated and began the pursuit of clarity and creation. I put away childish things. I became an adult—what a grand day in my spiritual growth when I discovered that I no longer needed adult supervision! I had something to say; I had something to contribute. I was a person with a body and a mind who had something wonderful to express—a spirit totally mine.

None of us need live like empty shells. Yet, countless thousands of people do seem to be doing just that. Let us constantly examine this Creation of God. Let us walk like a part of the Energy of God. Think and live like the spirit-mind-consciousness that we are. Let us know that we can charge our batteries at any time. How? By energizing our thoughts and recognizing ourselves as part of a great Universal Energy.

In years past, when I was in the bar business, a man would come into the establishment once a week to empty the juke box of its nickels (it was a long time ago, after all). I stood behind the bar watching this operation often. I do not know how many of you have had the opportunity to see the insides of a juke box. It is an incredible experience. It is such a fantastic creation of red, black, white and yellow wires—with hundreds of feet of wiring and scores of connections. However, in looking back on this time, I know that the juke box, as intricate as its design and manufacturing was, still had to be plugged into an electrical socket to make it work. Without that hook-up it also was a shell, unable to produce musical sound.

The human body is a magnificent instrument of God that knows just where everything is properly placed, each organ and cell having purpose and knowing its task. The juke box with all of its electrical arteries could never come close to the human body; it could never be compared to our digestive system, our intestinal tract, our sensory system, or our immune system. It could never be eyes, nor ears.

I would like to quote from Og Mandino's glorious little book, *The God Memorandum*. This is a simulated conversation between God and God's creation, man. God speaks:

> "Your brain is the most complex structure in the Universe. I know. Within its three pounds are fifteen billion nerve cells, more than three times as many cells as there are people on the earth.
>
> "To help you file away every perception, every sound, every taste, every smell, every action you have experienced since the day of your birth, I have implanted within your cells more than one thousand billion, billion protein molecules. Every incident in your life is there waiting only your recall. And, to assist your brain in the control of your body, I have dispersed, throughout your form, four million pain sensitive structures, five-hundred thousand touch detectors and more than two-hundred thousand temperature detectors. No nation's gold is better protected than you. None of your ancient wonders is greater than you.
>
> "You are my finest creation.
>
> "Within you is enough atomic energy to destroy any of the world's great cities...and rebuild them."

Batteries not included!

The batteries are awareness, perception, attitudes, feelings, thoughts. Yet what good are we if we are not connected to the One Source? How meaningless and meandering Life becomes when we are not connected to that One Divine Essence.

How empty we must be when we try to separate from this Divine Essence.

Mind is that which restores us in the "...valley of the shadow of death." Mind is that which charges us, regenerates us after we have reached the lowest ebb. But as Longfellow said, "The lowest ebb of the tide is the turn of the tide." I can remember when my tide turned, can you? Or has yours yet to turn up and out?

Unfortunately, so many of us try to live without this connection. Someone may ask of us the question, "Did you ever try to live without a spiritual connection?" If it were asked of me, my hand certainly would have to rise.

I say, facetiously but sincerely, that when I hooked up to the One Source, I became a "happy hooker." In the earlier part of my life, I fashioned it after French bread—one long loaf, especially when it came to using the power of my mind. Then, as I continued to refashion Life with affirmative thinking and constructive thoughts, my outside world changed because the inner world within me had changed. We all know, I'm certain, that a changed mind is a changed life.

"An unexamined life is not worth living," the great teacher Plato said.

How well I can relate to the statement of wisdom, for I have examined why my life was not working. Why was I unloved, unhappy, without wealth or health? But when I commenced to take responsibility for my own life experience, my mental examination began, the testing of my belief system started. Then, I was able to look at myself with some objectivity, almost like a doctor reading an X-ray. I was able to diagnose my own case and find most all the causes of the problems and diseases.

Believe me, it was quite a case to study. But I discovered that every time my life was not working, guess who was around? Me! When my life was in shambles, guess who was always there? Me!

In our personal evaluation of just who we are, what we are, and where we are going (and why we want to go there), we have to perform what some people might call a "check-up from the neck up." We look at the effect, that is, our present experience and behavior, then we examine the reactions we receive from others when in our presence. From this, we decide what is the cause of the experience, who caused the experience we see ourselves in, and who caused the reactions we received from others? Then we decide what we are going to do about it.

Are there some things rumbling about in our thoughts that are the cause of our present situation and brought the people who are in our life there? There may be some very good attitudes and thoughts that have provided us with our present situation. Then again. . . .

It is said that we are poor in pocket, not when we have nothing, but when we do nothing. There is always something one can do about one's situation—one's "effect."

If you believe there is nothing you can do about what you are and how you live—then you are absolutely right. The Law of Mind will go to work and produce just exactly what you believe at any given moment. Therefore, we must stimulate, activate, and generate our greatest treasure, our mind.

We can sit up and take notice of something, but we cannot keep on sitting. It would seem you have to step up to bat if you think you want to hit a home run. You cannot reach first base or home plate while sitting on the bench—of course, you may be one that just likes to cheer someone else on or feel it's best to let others have the home run. If we keep sitting on our laurels, all those principles and dreams will go to waste and we'll watch the world go by—it will!

Somewhere along the way we have to transpose an old thought: We are *not* a body using a mind; we *are* a mind using a body. Therefore, as we become involved with this thing called a living body, our physical body, the body of our affairs, must respond accordingly.

All of us have the same access to that Divine Energy of the Universe that is the battery. It is the recharger of our life, which is included in our package when we are born. But, as Dr. Holmes has stated in the textbook of this teaching, "The seed of freedom is planted in the innermost being of man, but like the Prodigal Son, man must make the great discovery for himself."

This Divine Spark, this Divine Energy is everywhere—present and available to everyone. It is that Essence that makes a flower turn toward it; that melts the snow on one side of the mountain but not on the other side; that turns a salad, a ham sandwich, or a glass of orange juice into fingernails and hair. That Energy directs all of the vitamin pills we consume to go to exactly the right place in our body where it is needed. Have you noticed that, when you take your vitamins, you never have to tell vitamin C where to go or vitamin E what it must do? The vitamin knows because the body and its parts draw the energy to it. There is an intelligence within them, and within us, which knows all.

Talk about knowingness! Remember the old television commercial of a few years ago. A little boy runs into his dad's office—who just happens to be a dentist—and happily screams, "Daddy, daddy, only one cavity!" And Daddy turns to the camera, smiles, and says, "It must be the Crest."

Very often we are like that boy. We have everything: a full set of teeth, a full set of brains. But still, there is that one cavity, that one area of our life that is incomplete and unfulfilled.

What is missing from our lives? What is our cavity?

Is there a large hole in our lives? Is our manipulation of others keeping people from being part of our life experiences? Is our need to control other people, including our children, our spouses, our loved ones, our employees, causing us to experience a cavity of loneliness?

Is our pride so encompassng as to be the one thing that we need not only to swallow, but to remove from our emotional, spiritual, and psychological intake? Is fear carving out a small but growing niche in our subjective minds, not allowing us to enter into new experiences or new worlds, new emotional charges? Fear may create a huge vacuum in our lives. It can create a safety zone, too, a comfort zone. It leaves a cavity, a pit that is bottomless, as huge as a not-so-grand canyon. That's called isolation.

The renowned psychiatrist, Carl Jung, once said that everyone at the age of thirty-five and over who came to see him to get help was seeking God. Notice, please, that Dr. Jung did not say every other one, or every third one—but everyone. That is some statement—ironically, that is exactly the age when

I did an about-face, a 180-degree turn, in the area of spirituality and religion.

Up to that time I had demonstrated "things." I had manifested cars, homes, trips, people, the many proverbials that seemed so very necessary as goals of Life. Yet, something was missing. The huge cavity in life was becoming larger, more evident. What was missing was love.

The absence of love created an enormous cavity in my life. Love was the battery that was always there; it was included. It was within me, but I didn't know it.

Once I found out I could love, I could then be loved. I could share and accept the sharing of others. I could care and be cared for. My light was turned up to high.

Love, God, the Divine Force, Energy, Essence, Mind, Universal Good, whatever you wish to call it, is included in each of us when we enter this exciting experience called Life. But as Stewart Emery wrote in his glorious book, *Actualizations*, "When we are born, we are handed a ticket to the show, but that does not guarantee us that we are going to enjoy it."

The whole thing is up to each of us. Self-examination, self-probing, self-inquiring into why our lives are empty, why there is no light, love, or laughter in life, can be the very first step to changing our lives.

In the first part of my own life, the first fifty years, I was like a chameleon—changing colors to match my environment. If the chameleon sits on a brown stone, he becomes brown in color. If the ground is a yellowish color, so also is the chameleon.

It was the same with me at that earlier time. If a person was of a certain religious or political party or belief, I would assume that very religion, party, and belief. I had a terror of offending people. I wanted to please everyone—quite a frustrating position for anyone to be in—because it is an impossibility.

Then I recognized that this attitude of being something for everyone but my own self was a crying out to everyone, "Please love me." I finally admitted to myself that love was the great void, the large vacuum in my life. When that recognition arrived on the scene, the facade that was Tom Costa (or B.C.) was lifted.

Love! Love of myself, love of God, love of others charged my life. And now that I know that, I consider it the most important thing in my life. I average about ten to a hundred "I love you's" each and every day. Let us think of the words of another song: "I Had It All The Time!"

Love is included in the energy package called "me."

Love is included in the energy package called "you."

11

Author! Author!

I love theater.

In fact, one of the restaurant-bars I owned was named "The Backstage." The entrance to the restaurant was actually the backstage of the Ivar Theater in Hollywood, just around the corner from the famous intersection, Hollywood and Vine. The Ivar was somewhat like an off-Broadway theater, and several now-famous stars began their careers on that stage before going into films.

Theater was always very important in my life when I lived in Hollywood. It certainly is a part of my life now that I live in the desert. Here, in the Coachella Valley, surrounded by mountains from Palm Springs to Indio, and Palm Desert to Thousand Palms and Desert Hot Springs, we have a stage on which a thousand dramas are played daily.

If you are a theatergoer, you know what happens the opening night of a play. There is that feeling of excitement, like the birth of a baby. The author has been incubating his plot, the lines for the characters, and the theme and intent of his play over a long period of time. Now the opportunity to bring it into a live being is at hand. His idea and his application of talent is now bearing fruit.

If anyone has had the opportunity to be backstage at an opening night of a play or musical, they can tell you about the butterflies in the minds and hearts of actors, actresses, stagehands, and, of course, the director and the author.

And, if it is a new play, on or off-Broadway, or in Boston, Washington, or Hollywood, there is that memorable moment that happens sometimes in a writer's life. After the curtain calls for the players, there begins a cry from the audience, "Author! Author!"

The Author (now with a capital "A") hears the thunderous applause of approval. Probably, after a reasonable amount of clapping and shouting, the Author rushes down the aisle, jumps upon the stage, and steps before the footlights to receive the acknowledgment and acceptance of the opening-night audience. Success!

At long last a particular moment of acceptance is achieved for his dramatic presentation. The playwright is as moved as is the audience by the theater experience. Probably the acclaim will mean a long run for the work. If it was first presented outside of New York City, it might move to a greater production, perhaps even Broadway—the epitome of acceptance.

But it isn't always true.

I recall the Los Angeles opening night of *Kismet*. It was not acceptable to the critics, nor the audience. There was no standing ovation for actors, nor a shout for the playwright and musicians. There were no good reviews; many critics said it would not last a week. *Kismet* lasted a good deal longer than a week and went on to Broadway. There, its opening night took place during a newspaper strike. The only criticism that could be detected was by Brooks Atkinson, who, an hour after curtain, read his review over *The New York Times* radio station WQXR, and he was not at all kind. It didn't matter, no one was hearing the review. With no printed criticism and review, the audiences did not know they were seeing a very "poor musical drama." During the more than two years it ran they enjoyed the beautiful music and nightly called the performers and the creators to the footlights. *Kismet*, with popular music fashioned from the classic melodies of the composer, Borodin, is a theater classic, and it is still presented throughout the country.

Now, how does all this apply to you and me?

The answer is quite simple, really. We are the author, producer, director, and the star of our ongoing autobiography. Often, we call in a cast of hundreds to play in our melodrama entitled, *My Life!*

Can you recall your first day in kindergarten or first grade? Perhaps you remember more easily your first day in high school or college, the first day of your first job. Remember your wedding—your FIRST wedding, that is! Or remember your first child's birth? Your first loss through death? These are certainly dramatic, even traumatic moments in our play of Life. And no one stars in any of these events, but we ourselves.

All the various scenes with the ever-changing scenery, the backdrops, our kitchens, our living rooms, our offices. The scenarios, the asides (or life's digressions) to the audiences—all are authored by us.

Some years ago, in a restaurant where I was working, I had a conversation with that wonderful playwright, William Saroyan. He directed my attention to a busboy cleaning the dishes off a nearby table. "See that young man," he said. "If a good playwright would write about all the 'things' that have happened to *him* up to this moment, and it was written well, it could be an Oscar winner."

I have not forgotten that, for I acknowledge in my own experiences there were some heavy scenes (some of which I have touched upon earlier). The plot thickened many times before the final curtain fell on those earlier episodes of my life.

Life! You Wanna Make Something of It?

I like to use the word "episode." It's a word I like to employ when I find myself in the midst of a situation or a condition. I refer to the problem itself as an "episode." The very word means an "incident," a "scene"—a brief unit of action in a dramatic work. When I refer to the present as an episode, whether problematic or not, it means that I subjectively believe and accept that "This too shall pass." Anything that is taking place has one permanent result at the outset: There is an end to the action, to the problem. It is merely an episode in life, an occurrence, an incident that has a beginning and also an ending.

We all have a life story. We are all authors, producers, stars of our own story, our play. Some of us, of course, are still play-acting; some of us keep calling in the large casts and chorus to play in our opera, whether "soapy" or not.

What happened to you during this past week could be written into a three-act grand stage play. What took place with you last night could be a dramatic episode, a poignant scene in a play.

Author means "creator." It means the maker, the originator, the parent, the one who fathers. Therefore, applying that idea to our lives on a universal basis, God is the Creator, the One Source, the Maker, the Father. But the creation of your individual life begins with what you personally, individually choose to have dramatized—and brought into action.

Dr. Frederic Bailes, the great New Age teacher (*Your Mind Can Heal You*) spoke of the idea of "parent thoughts." An ancient word for "father" is derived from the French, *de sire*. This means that our desire, our point of focus, is chosen as the selector of ideas. We place that chosen idea into the

Mother Womb of the Universe. What results is the "baby." Dr. Bailes also says that we have many offsprings of jealousy and of hate—also insecurity because we have parented those thoughts.

Someone has stated that all books of fiction, all television comedies and dramas, all films and plays have one theme: that is, of getting into trouble and getting out of trouble. The scenes that immediately flash into my mind are *Love Boat* sequences. It seems that all the episodes of that series are based on "Hello, I love you. I hate you. I love you. Goodbye."

So when we watch a situation-comedy on television, you'll know what I mean if you watch *The Jeffersons*, *The Golden Girls*, *Three's Company*—any of them—the main characters get into trouble so that thirty minutes later they can get out of trouble. Every one of the *I Love Lucy* series episodes are certainly based upon that one theme. The difference between these shows and our own non-fiction situation-comedy is that it takes us a lot longer than thirty minutes to get out of trouble. For some of us it takes thirty or forty years!

In Genesis, chapter one, everything was good; "...lo, it was very good." Then in Genesis two, we got into trouble. We were tossed out of the Garden of Eden, and it seems to me like the remainder of the Bible is attempting to get us back into the completeness of Genesis one. But is this not the basis for all prayer? We desire to return to that wholeness, that completeness. We want to return to where we were before the situation began. Back to where we never had it so good.

So whether it is the Bible, Genesis one, or our own life, we must accept responsibility for whatever we have written on the tablet of Life, the one entitled *My Life.* Whether we are aware or not, we authorize whatever *has* happened to us, whatever *is* happening to us—and certainly what *will* happen to us. We allow all the clothes, the cars, the money, the friends and the non-friends, the whatever is, to come into our experience.

In the word "authority" is the word "author." Comforting? What that means to me is that when we allow something to enter into our experience, we authorize it to come in. We acknowledge its presence. Therefore, we are the author of that page in our book, that scene, that episode, that good or bad experience.

But just as an author is able to rewrite a book, the play, the scenario, so too can we. We may edit, re-edit and rewrite, change, alter, or delete the characters. As author, we can change the environment of the drama, the comedy, the tragedy, the disaster—and at any time we so choose. So if we believe we cannot change it, then not a word of dialogue and not one scene, not one aspect can be altered. We are, then, stuck in that script of our life.

Can we change the script? Can we choose another kind of episode for our participation? It may be comedy or it may be as "sad as any Russian play could guarantee." It could be a "zippity doo-da script" or one of outrageous fortune.

> *(I have an actress friend who once confided to me that, when she was doing a comedy onstage or in a film, her life took on a light, airy atmosphere. Life was fun, just as it was for the character of the play she was performing. However, when playing a heavy role, a Medea, her life would almost match the tragic feeling of that role.)*

154

When you are "playing a role" in life, there is a part of you that does not know you are onstage, in a film, or in your own home. I remember one member of Alcoholics Anonymous saying to me that, when he was uptight, nervous, even fearful, he reverted to a more peaceful state, even temporarily, when he acted "as if" he were calm, confident, and casual. And if he progressed long enough in the "role" he became that very feeling. Then he could deal with the causation of his temporary plight.

To authorize means to "sanction, to justify, to furnish grounds for, to commission, to give license to." So, I ask the question, what have we sanctioned as being true in our life's story? Some questions could be: What have we justified? What have we commissioned to be the theme of our life? And what tragedy or comedy in us have we furnished grounds for?

Mother Teresa, as a self-proclaimed pencil in God's hand, has written "service to mankind." She has written love; she has written dedication and commitment. Let us add to the acknowledgment and the acclaim of the Nobel Peace Prize Committee, and applaud her life shouting, "*Brava*, Mother Teresa." Let us shout "*Encore, s'il vous plait.*" She has created and authorized a life of good, of God, of sharing, caring, and giving of herself. She could have written something else on her sheet of life paper—she chose not to.

Personally, I do not believe in the Judgment Day. But let us think about our justice on that particular day, fantasize about that idea. Let us think of our last day as a human being. Would there be acknowledgment of all we have done on earth, a spiritual ovation, crying "Author Author!" Would there be plaudits and praises for our actions, our deeds and accomplishments, our achievements? I have asked myself this question. I think it is a valid one to ask ourselves.

The message I received upon examining my feelings about this is that, if I do not feel there would be a clamoring of "Author, Author," then this is the moment I can change the script. This is the minute I can change the scenery. At this moment I may change the dialogue, the theme and the intent of my life. We can alter the characters in our play. We can rebuild the backdrop, the scenery—anytime we choose.

The beginning of any alteration is to know that it is possible to change something. It is quite possible to rewrite a script, to rewrite the words, to delete some of the "things" we have authorized for the actor in our life script. We change the things by changing thoughts.

Are we not the authors who authorized the judgment that we find so painful, the prejudice that keeps us from growing? Did we not cause the isolation that imprisons us in our mental cell, our rejection that helps us stay in the past? Are we not quite responsible for the history of our hurts, our resentments and regrets?

We revise the script because we authored the first draft. We look at what we authorized to help us go in a certain direction—not where we do not want to go.

It is not unlike a man sailing his boat. If the wind is not blowing in the direction he desires to go, he does not sit on the shore drumming his fingers, waiting for a change of wind. What does he do? He changes his relationship to the wind, by what is called "tacking." He uses the wind, which is actually blowing against him. He uses it so that he can sail in the direction he chooses to go. Is this not what we do when we offer prayer? Is this not what we do when we meditate?

We can center ourselves, no matter what "ill wind" is blowing against us.

So, as the person sailing his boat by tacking into the wind, we have to change our tactics, our relationship to the Universe, and to ourselves. It is said that the same wind that tosses you about on the sea is the very wind that helps you into a safe port. Every experience is a completed idea, whether it is a day out at sea, a day in the office, or a day on your job. Stop for a moment, put down the book, and think about this: Every experience is a completed idea.

We need to watch our ideas—even guard them. Those things we dwell upon in thought are quite likely to become our new situation or the latest condition, the up-to-the-moment effect of the mental cause set into motion. Instead, watch your ideas become solutions. Observe ideas as they become answers.

Ideas cause our problems, therefore ideas are the solution to our problems.

When you put down this book today, realize that you ARE the author of your life story. Then, author the ideas so that when they do come to fruition your life is enriched, your life is enhanced. So, too, are the lives of those surrounding you.

We are masters at the practice of degrading ourselves, demoralizing and debilitating ourselves. We dwell upon what is wrong with us rather than what is right. We are such great students learning how to blame everything on the other person. We spend such a great deal of time "awfulizing." This practice is common. It is heard in markets, restaurants, standing in line at the bank, the movie, whatever: "Isn't it awful?" "Isn't she awful?" "Isn't he awful?" "Now, isn't Awful awful?"

Stop the *awful* awfulizing!

There is a saying that each time a sheep bleats, it misses a mouthful of hay. That idea cured me of a lot of awfulizing. Awfulizing stunts your spiritual and emotional growth. You cannot grow if you are still bemoaning how unfair Life is, how truly awful Life treats you. Actually, the way you tell a dead flower from a live one is to see if it is growing!

Ask yourself today, "What is the theme of the play I am now play-acting? " The title may be the same, *My Life,* but is the theme altering? Is the background music still filled with sad songs, old dirges of the past? Or is the music lighter, more airy, happy? Is my life story filled with pathos or with comedy?

Whatever or whichever it is, remember it is we who author the play. When we arrive at the end of the wonderful trail of our life or to the conclusion of a productive day, can the Father within say, "This is my beloved, in whom I am well pleased?"

Or, "What a blessed life my beloved one has authored! What a blessed day, what a blessed week, what a blessed year, my beloved son or daughter has experienced."

Can you, with the One Creator, say, "Good show!" "*C'est magnifique!*" Or even "Author! Author!"

What we can desire for ourselves at several points of the play titled *My Life* is to be able to step to the footlights, bow and simply say, "Thank you. Thank you."

Afterword

Acknowledgment is one of the greater traits that we as human beings can develop. So, in my acknowledging the completion and the event of this book of essays, I realize how very many, many people have contributed to its creation. Literally, if you will, this book has been sixty-six years in the making. So, listing all of the contributors to my life and the life of this collection of ideas would be to take up countless pages leaving very little room for the message.

However, there are a few who stand out as the helpers, the prodders, the supporters in my ministerial life, whom I wish to acknowledge with great feelings of gratitude. First of all, there is Dr. Ernest Holmes, the founder of our glorious teaching, Science of Mind. Without him this book could not have been written. My ministry would have never happened in the way that it did.

Along the pathway are some of my mentors, my teachers, such as Dr. Earl Barnum, Reverend Harold Jones, Dr. Robert H. Bitzer, Dr. Raymond Charles Barker, Dr. Catherine Ponder, Dr. William Taliaferro, Dr. Frank Richelieu.

Gratitude I give to Harry Foxworth—and praise and thankfulness to all of my colleagues and fellow ministers of both Religious Science International and the United Church of Religious Science. To all the New Thought leaders in this growing and viable movement, I give thanks for dedication and service.

I wish to thank, with love, my entire congregation of Church of Religious Science of the Desert, in

Life! You Wanna Make Something of It?

Palm Desert, California. I wish to express my deep appreciation for support to all those who were with me right from the very start of my ministry in 1973. And to all of those who along the way have loved, supported, and helped me, I say once again, "Thank you." My recognition and thanks also to the countless number of ushers, the many dependable members of the board of trustees, and all those musicians, the singers, the people who worked in the office, the bookstore helpers, the Sunday school teachers, and those who have helped in the formation of this great church.

A special and personal acknowledgment to Louise L. Hay and Hay House, Inc., for their belief in me and the publication of this text. And hearty thanks to my editor, Warren Bayless.

And to you, dear readers, my deep respect, esteem, and gratitude; I bless you (without delay) for your desire to make something of your life.

I acknowledge all of you. I salute all of you.

—Dr. Tom Costa